GENUINE PIZZA

GENUINE PIZZA

**better pizza
at home**

**by
michael
schwartz**

JAMES BEARD AWARD-WINNING CHEF

WITH
OLGA MASSOV

PHOTOGRAPHS BY
SIDNEY BENSIMON

ABRAMS, NEW YORK

contents

RECIPE LIST

As a chef who not only played a big role in popularizing gourmet artisanal pizza in the United States but also gave a job to Michael Schwartz in the early days of his professional cooking career, I am honored to share a few words here about *Genuine Pizza*.

That word "genuine" perfectly sums up what Michael and his approach to cooking in general—and more specifically to cooking pizza—are all about. His restaurants and hospitality company not only have genuine in their name, but they also feature genuine ingredients and serve food that is genuinely cooked and genuinely delicious. So it makes perfect sense that Michael's personal motto is: "The secret to good food is good food."

Even before he came up with that simple expression that says it all, I could tell that Michael was a genuine guy. I could tell that Michael simply got it when he first joined the kitchen at my Chinois on Main restaurant in Santa Monica, where my team and I developed what came to be known as Asian fusion cuisine, combining Chinese tradition with California ingredients and contemporary French techniques. He understood the importance of using only fresh, in-season, local produce, seafood, and other ingredients, combining them in ways that highlighted their natural flavors and textures.

And then, as he charmingly shares in his introduction to this book, he actually first learned to make pizza in a quick tutorial from the chef at the Tokyo branch of my Spago restaurant. That was the spark that exploded into Michael's enduring passion for pizza, which eventually gave rise to his Genuine Pizza restaurants.

Every page of this book with that same name impresses me. Michael's approach to pizza combines classical discipline, a dedication to using the best ingredients, and high-flying yet sensible creativity. He shows special dedication to helping home cooks achieve results as good as what he serves in his restaurant.

It all starts with his explanation of pizza-making technique. His instructions for making pizza dough, and his basic recipe, as well as others for a rye dough and a gluten-free dough, are extremely helpful and foolproof. I'm especially impressed with the logical chart he offers of a pizza's basic elements, and his guidelines for putting them together smartly.

Then there are the pizzas themselves. To put it simply, every recipe in this book makes my mouth water, especially in combination with photographs that look hot-from-the-oven and beautiful. (I also have to add that, based on those photos, Michael knows how to cook a pizza the way I like it, with a crispy, bubbly, very well-browned crust.) Among so many options, his Mushroom Pizza; Short Rib Pizza with Caramelized Onions, Gruyère, and Arugula; Shrimp Pizza with Roasted Lemon, Scallion, and Cilantro; Fennel Pizza with Caramelized Onion and Green Olives; Bacon, Egg, and Cheese Pizza; and Pastrami on Rye Pizza make me want to get in the kitchen and cook.

That doesn't even begin to touch on his imaginative recipe section on Things to Eat with Your Pizza. His recipes (and photos) for dishes all seem irresistible, from Meatballs to Homemade Ricotta; White Bean and Chorizo Soup to Escarole Salad with Lemon, Anchovy, Parmigiano-Reggiano, and Breadcrumbs; Roasted Chicken with Salsa Verde and Fennel Slaw to Slow-Roasted Pork Shoulder with Soft Polenta and Shaved Celery Salad; Buttermilk Panna Cotta with a variety of fruit compote toppings to Dark Chocolate Cremoso with Candied Orange Peel, Soft Cream, and Pine Nuts; plus a variety of easy, imaginative cocktails.

From first page to last, *Genuine Pizza* feels inspired. I hope it inspires you to create many wonderful home-cooked meals.

—Wolfgang Puck

let's make pizza at home

We're currently experiencing something of an artisanal pizza renaissance, with more excellent pizzerias dedicated to perfecting the craft of pizza-making popping up now than ever before. More and more people are paying attention not just to the quality of their dough, but also to the toppings, sourcing everything with great care. They're building customized pizza ovens, curing their own charcuterie, using wild fermentation for their dough, and obsessing over every detail—all in order to deliver pizza perfection to you. The craft of pizza has never been more advanced.

That said, even though one's life work can easily be dedicated to perfecting pizza, I firmly believe that you, the home cook reading this, can make truly excellent pizza in your own kitchen. While you may lack the specialty oven that cooks your pizza in mere minutes, blasting heat of somewhere around 900°F (482°C), you can still wind up with wonderful results using the oven in your kitchen. In addition to eating well, you'll have a lot of fun making it. My goal with this book is to convince you that not only *can* you make excellent pizza at home, but that you *should*, and you'll enjoy doing it.

I've always believed that good food starts with good ingredients, and that the secret to good food is good food. Few things in my mind exemplify this philosophy as much as pizza. With so few ingredients, pizza is both simple and complex, pedestrian and highbrow. Its universal appeal lies in its accessibility, and while it's essentially dough with toppings, pizza happens to be a food just about everyone likes. It can be as humble as you want or as luxurious as you want—there's no limit to the craft.

I also love pizza for its convivial nature: Pizza is meant to be shared, it invites a crowd, it fosters conversation. It's the beginning of—or part of—a delicious meal, and as you read through the book, you will see that I believe in pairing pizza with other dishes to balance out the spread. One can't live on pizza alone, and so I also share some of the dishes we offer to our patrons at Genuine Pizza: starters, soups, salads—and even desserts and drinks.

But how did I get into cooking and, more specifically, become so obsessed with pizza?

I grew up in Philadelphia eating shitty pizza, and my thoughts on pizza were not particularly profound. It was there. I ate it. My dad owned an auto supply shop, and as a teen I would spend my summers stocking shelves. At some point when I was in high school, my dad decided that it was time for me to get a real job. We got in the car and he drove me to one of the fanciest restaurants in Philly, DiLullo, known for serving progressive Italian food (which was unusual, as most places serving Italian food were red sauce joints). I wore a shirt and tie, and went in to ask for a job. To my surprise, they gave me one on the spot—I started as a busboy that night. I worked my way up the ranks, and eventually became their lead line cook.

Working in the kitchen appealed to me in so many ways. I loved the pace, the environment, the high pressure of it all. As a teen, I loved being part of this adult world, and I realized I was actually good at cooking—it came naturally to me, and it gave me focus. When you're an adolescent, realizing that you're good at something is an immensely empowering thing. I felt capable and I wanted to learn more.

Early on, I realized that college wasn't for me. I didn't get into the cooking apprenticeship program at my local community college, and after taking a few business classes (and being incredibly bored), I dropped out altogether. I never did wind up going to cooking school.

Eventually, I found myself working for Wolfgang Puck at Chinois in Santa Monica, California. Wolfgang and his approach to cooking—fresh and vibrant—made me think about flavors in a whole different way; it opened my mind to so many different possibilities. Wolfgang was one of the pioneers of California cuisine, teaching us, his cooks, to think about local in-season produce, and coaxing flavor out of what was around us.

I had been working at Chinois for about a year, and the Japanese chefs I was working with there connected me with some chefs who were opening a California-style restaurant in Japan. Those chefs invited me to come to Japan and do a consultation on what a California-style restaurant should be—part of which was to teach a pizza class. I had zero idea what that meant; I had never made a pizza from scratch at that time. But Wolfgang had a Spago in Tokyo and I figured maybe I could pick up a few pointers while there. The night before I had to teach that class I got a quick pizza-making tutorial from a Tokyo-based Spago chef, Serge: the dough, the toppings, the baking. I showed up, and pretending to be a pizza expert, taught the class on the fly, acting like I was born slinging pies. Much to my surprise—and relief—the class went very well. Everyone seemed to think that I knew what I was talking about. I must've looked pretty authoritative.

Though I was new to the whole pizza thing, I was instantly hooked: I loved the process of making the dough. I loved how it felt in my hands—how it changed with time as I allowed it to rise and bubble up. That the dough was alive, growing, and changing before my eyes, fascinated me. I was amazed that while it was relatively easy to make a decent pizza from scratch, you could keep working at it and working at it, perfecting the craft, your whole life.

Eventually, a little while after I had my first restaurant, Michael's Genuine Food and Drink, in Miami, we started thinking about opening another one that specialized in pizza. We had a pizza program at the restaurant, and it was quite popular. But we wanted to dedicate more resources to it. We wanted a place that served great pizza, using quality ingredients, where everything—from the crust to the garnishes—was carefully considered.

From the time I taught that class in Japan, I had been in love with pizza making, but now I wanted to explore the art of it more seriously. After some planning and working on the dough recipe, we finally had a formula we were happy with. And in 2011, our original pizzeria, Harry's (named for my son), opened its doors. It became a popular, beloved neighborhood spot, and eventually we grew the concept bigger, expanding to open several locations of a new restaurant, Genuine Pizza, around the Miami area. We were able to scale up our method to carefully consider every ingredient and part of the process, and I'm so proud of what the team and I created.

In the process of sharing recipes in this book, I am also highlighting my cooking philosophy: In my restaurants, using one single dish or preparation in as many different recipes as possible allows for running a more efficient kitchen, and nowhere is this resourcefulness more desired, I think, than in the kitchens of busy home cooks. Another term for this is "batch cooking," which allows you to create building blocks for the week in order to put meals together in a short amount of time. Success in the kitchen is partially dependent on stocking an arsenal of pantry staples, and learning simple preparations that will do the work of building and rounding out your meals. Sauces, dressings, pickled things—these can be applied across many types of dishes, so any time you can make a bigger batch of something and use it several ways, you'll be rewarded in spades. Slow roast some short ribs (see page 197) for dinner one night, throw some leftover ribs in the soup (see page 157) the following evening, and on the third night, take a few bits of that leftover beef to make pizza (see page 79).

My promise to you is simple: If you follow the recipes in this book, you will become a better cook. And you'll eat some delicious things in the process. That's my guarantee.

THE BUILDING BLOCKS AND WHAT YOU NEED TO KNOW BEFORE YOU START

THE BASICS

EQUIPMENT

To make pizza, you need a few tools to help you along the way. There's a good chance you already own most of the tools listed here, but I wanted to mention them to be thorough and complete. Who knows, maybe you own pizza peels but not a kitchen scale? Most of the items are not costly and shouldn't set you back much. They are also utilitarian and, with proper care, will last you a lifetime.

Bench scraper—These inexpensive tools present in every professional kitchen are useful for cutting dough and scraping its remains off your counter. They are also handy when transporting large amounts of chopped ingredients from one place (say, your cutting board) to another (a pan).

Blender—If you have a standing blender, great—it is a workhorse and will effortlessly puree larger batches of soup, salad dressing, and tomato sauce. If you've got the funds, spring for a professional-strength blender, such as a Vitamix, which will last you a lifetime and will be a good investment. Otherwise, an immersion blender (page 20) will serve you beautifully.

Box grater—Essential when you need to coarsely grate cheese or vegetables, box graters are inexpensive and last forever.

Deli containers in quart (L) and pint (480 ml) sizes—Incredibly useful for storing food. No chef can go without them, and I'm on a mission to make them a must-have in your kitchen, as well. You can either collect take-out containers, or you can purchase a bunch, for next to nothing, online. They come in pint (L) and quart (480 ml) sizes and are simply great. Clear, so you can see what's inside them, and stackable. You can also get them at restaurant supply stores.

Deli container labels (e.g. blue painter's tape and a Sharpie permanent marker)—How else are you going to label your deli containers? Label the container with the date and what's inside it, and you will never again wonder about the contents and how long it's been in there.

Digital scale—If you're still on the fence about whether or not you really need a kitchen scale, let me be emphatic—you *do*. In pizza making, particularly when it comes to dough, precise measurements are important to help you get to a great result. Of course, there are other outside factors that will affect the outcome of the recipe—experience will help you perfect the practice—but whereas a measurement of flour using the scoop-and-sweep method will vary vastly depending on how compacted your flour is, weight in grams is weight in grams, and will stay precise. You can get a great digital scale for under $30 and it will truly transform how you cook. They don't require much space for storage, and I've never met anyone who regretted adding it to their kitchen arsenal.

Food mill—On the one hand, it might seem silly to suggest having something as singularly focused as a food mill, but I've yet to find a better way to process whole canned tomatoes into a smooth sauce with some texture. You can use the mill for apple sauce or butter, mashed potatoes, and much, much more.

Grill and/or pizza oven—I've used Lynx grills and pizza ovens for years, and they make, by far, the most excellent equipment. However, they are quite an investment, and at the end of the day, you can make excellent pizza using any grill or pizza oven.

Immersion blender—Every kitchen should have an immersion blender. They're cheap, quick, easy, and effective. They're also not as much of a commitment space-wise as standing blenders, and are easy to clean and store. They're useful for making soups, vinaigrettes, sauces, mayonnaise, and more.

Mandoline—Even if your knife skills are exceptional, to get consistently perfect paper-thin slices of zucchini (see page 131) or evenly sliced pear (see page 165), you will need a mandoline. A good one. I like Benriner—it's about $20, and outside of inexpensive blade replacements from time to time, it should last awhile. Please exercise caution when using a mandoline, as it is extremely sharp.

Microplane grater/zester—While other zesters tend to pull and rip the citrus skin, Microplane's sharp, precise microblades will get you just the zest with no pith. Great not only for zesting citrus, Microplane excels at creating beautiful, fluffy shavings of cheese and chocolate. It will grate garlic (which is easier and less messy than mincing), and it's fantastic for grating nutmeg. Affordable and made to last, it is, in my opinion, the only fine grater worth spending money on, and a must in any kitchen.

Oven thermometer—Oven thermometers (another inexpensive item for your kitchen) come in handy for revealing the precise temperature inside your oven. No matter how expensive and high quality, no oven is perfect, and when it comes to baking and roasting, it's useful to know if your oven runs hot or cool—and by how much. Depending on whichever way your oven goes, you may want to cook your pizza (or other food) for a longer or shorter amount of time.

Pepper mill—Freshly ground black pepper is really important, because pre-ground black pepper is always stale. There's a pepper mill I'm obsessed with—the Unicorn—and it can easily be found online. If I could afford to get each home cook one, I would.

Pizza ovens—These days, there are myriad pizza oven options out there, from multi-thousand-dollar, custom-built outdoor models to inexpensive countertop versions for indoor kitchens. These pizza ovens tend to get hotter than the 500°F (260°C) regular ovens do, which makes them better at making pizza. Because our dough has oil and honey in it, 1000°F (538°C) is too high for our pizzas, but anywhere between 550°F (288°C) to 750°F (399°C) makes for ideal baking temperatures. You can also warm a pizza stone (see opposite) on a grill and cook your pizza with the grill cover down (that gets you to the right temperature as well). The hotter the cooking environment (within the parameters I describe above), the better!

Pizza peels—I know what I'm about to say might raise some eyebrows, but you need two pizza peels for the easiest, smoothest pizza-at-home process: a wooden one to put your pizza in the oven (the raw dough doesn't stick to the wood), and a stainless-steel peel (say that three times fast), which allows you to easily transport your pizza from the oven to the cutting board.

Pizza stone—A must if you want to make pizza at home, a pizza stone will help you evenly cook your pizza crust to perfection. For best results, heat the pizza stone well in advance, and be sure to give enough time for the stone to thoroughly warm up before making your pizza—at least 30 minutes at 500°F (260°C).

Pizza wheel—A pizza wheel lets you cut your pizza into precise slices with ease. Trying to do it with a knife will be far less effective, as it's hard to hold the hot crust with one hand while trying to cut your pizza with the other.

Plastic bowl scraper—These flexible scrapers will get every bit of dough out of your bowl, which will also make it much easier to clean the bowl once you're done using it.

Probe thermometer—Not necessary for making pizza, or most recipes in this book, but I wanted to throw this kitchen tool in because I find probe thermometers immensely useful in the kitchen and they will make you a better cook. No more well-done steak meant to be medium-rare! Precision—and perfectly cooked proteins—will be yours. While Thermapens are the undisputed coveted probe thermometers, you can get by with a cheaper brand, such as ThermoPro, which retails for less than $10 on Amazon and will still get you great results.

Silicone spatulas—When purchasing spatulas, make sure they are made of silicone (and not plastic), so that they don't melt when exposed to high heat. Useful in getting every bit of batter or dough out of the bowl, these spatulas are also great for stirring ingredients while they are cooking. If you get the ones made entirely out of silicone, you can even throw them in your dishwasher.

Stainless-steel bowls—Cheap and indestructible, stainless-steel bowls are the workhorses of restaurant kitchens—and every home cook should have a few on hand. Go to a restaurant supply shop, where you'll get the best bang for your buck, and buy a few bowls in varying sizes. I guarantee you: You'll use them forever.

Vegetable Y-peeler—Aside for peeling vegetables (the task that gave this tool its name), these Y-shaped peelers are also great for shaving hard cheeses or making vegetable ribbons (think carrots or zucchini).

Wooden and metal mixing spoons—No kitchen is complete without these. Use them for mixing dough or stirring sauces and soup.

PANTRY

A useful pantry does not need to be complicated; a few simple and easy-to-find ingredients will take your recipes far. If you take care to seek out quality basics, they will, in turn, make your pizza (and other dishes) taste that much better.

Active dry yeast—At the restaurant we use fresh yeast, but all the pizza recipes in this book have been tested using active dry yeast as it's easier for a home cook to procure.

Anchovies—Many people will tell me they dislike anchovies, but more often than not, it turns out that's because they've had only mediocre ones. Seek out quality anchovies, as this will really make a difference, especially anywhere the anchovy is left whole. The best anchovies are packed in salt, but there are some good oil-packed brands, such as Agostino Recca.

Bacon—You don't need to add a lot to get some nice flavor, so try to find a good quality, nitrate-free, slow-smoked bacon. I like Niman Ranch brand for their progressive, sustainable approach to farming and raising animals (not to mention that the product tastes incredible as a result), and it's widely available.

Bread flour—We prefer to use bread flour for our pizza dough (as opposed to all-purpose flour) because of its higher protein content, which produces a dough with more chew. In my opinion, more chew equals a more satisfying-tasting crust. We like King Arthur flour for its quality and consistency.

Calabrian chiles—You can find crushed Calabrian chiles in oil online or in specialty shops, and though they're not available at every grocery store, they're very much worth seeking out. A small amount will add spicy, smoky, and salty flavors, and they are great as a pizza topping, an addition to sauces and salad dressings, or to bring some heat to any dish of your choosing.

Canned tomatoes—Always use whole canned tomatoes and then process them as needed, be it by chopping or pureeing. Canned diced tomatoes have added calcium chloride to help them keep their shape, so they don't break down properly during cooking. Find a brand you really like; Muir Glen is a great, widely available label.

Canola oil—This oil is great for deep-frying and any dish where you want the oil flavor to be neutral and not olive-y.

Cheese—Throughout this book, I use lots of different cheeses. Melting cheeses like Fontina and Gruyère; funky, creamy cheese like Taleggio; mild, creamy cheeses like mozzarella or *stracciatella*; and hard, salty cheeses, perfect for finishing pizza, like Parmigiano-Reggiano, Pecorino-Romano, or Grana Padano. As you continue to make pizza, you will figure out your own favorite cheeses to use, and I encourage you to experiment. Something like blue cheese may be unexpected, but it sure works when combined with an ingredient like peaches.

Crushed red pepper—These dried red chile flakes will add a spicy kick to anything that you feel requires it, from finishing off pizzas to salad dressings. A little goes a long way, so start with a pinch and build from there. Fresh crushed red pepper flakes are a bright, saturated red. If yours are a dull, dusty red, you may need to buy a fresh batch.

Extra-virgin olive oil—We make our pizza dough with some olive oil (a nod to Wolfgang Puck), and good olive oil is indispensable in any kitchen. From dressing salads to sautéing vegetables, olive oil is a necessity. I recommend having one on hand that you don't mind cooking with, and another one for finishing and dressing the dishes (where you can really taste the oil). Find the best-quality extra-virgin olive oil and use that.

Fresh herbs—Unless a recipe says otherwise, the herbs I use are fresh, as I like their bright flavor. Throughout this book you'll see lots of different kinds: parsley, dill, cilantro, rosemary, thyme, just to name a few.

Freshly ground black pepper—There is no comparison between pre-ground black pepper and freshly ground. The aroma of the latter is intoxicating, and the former always smells a little stale.

Honey—For the purposes of making pizza dough, you're looking for a honey that's light in color, as it will be the most mild tasting.

Lager-style beer—Because we make pizza on a larger scale at the restaurants, we could not use naturally fermented starters for our dough, but we really like the idea of *biga* (a prefermentation mixture added to dough for greater taste complexity), and so we add a little beer to our dough for its water content and that similar malty, yeasty flavor.

Olives—Never buy canned olives. Buy them in small amounts, as they tend to go bad relatively quickly. I like lots of different types, but the ones used most often in this book are Castelvetrano, Cerignola, and Kalamata.

Onions—Inexpensive and with a long shelf life, onions are an indispensable staple of just about every pantry, including mine. From chopping raw onions into salads, to slowly caramelizing them (see page 58) to use as a pizza topping, onions are essential to build complex flavor. When they are in season, typically in the summer months, I prefer to use the Georgia-grown Vidalia onions. They are milder and sweeter, and are absolutely worth seeking out.

Salts—In this book we call for two types of salt: kosher and flaky sea salt. For kosher salt, we use the Diamond Crystal brand, and for flaky sea salt, we like Maldon; both are widely available.

Smoked and cured meats—Having smoked and cured meats, such as bacon, spicy *soppressata*, or *prosciutto cotto* (and many others), in your refrigerator means not only having great snacking options but also flavor bombs. Adding these ingredients to pizzas, salads, and soups will enhance the dishes with a meaty, smoky flavor.

Whole-wheat flour—Adding a little bit of whole-wheat flour to the dough allows for more structure. It also gives the dough a slightly earthier flavor.

THE DOUGH

Pizza dough is a funny thing; with so few ingredients, it is simple to learn to make, but also takes a lifetime to master. There is no trick to crafting good pizza dough besides practice. Spend some time making batches of dough, and get a feel for the texture and the process. It's an elemental method, and while it won't take you very long to get quite good, you can spend a lifetime perfecting your pizza dough game. Just ask some dedicated *pizzaioli* who've spent—and continue to spend—their lives obsessing over dialing it in with their dough. Just as with all super-fundamental and basic things, dough's simplicity is also what makes it so elusive in the search for perfection. But master the crust, and you're 80 percent of the way to making delicious pizza.

There are several different types of pizza dough out there, the most famous being the original Neapolitan dough, with nothing but flour, yeast, water, and salt. There's also neo-Neapolitan, or New York–style dough, with the same ingredients as Neapolitan dough, plus the addition of olive oil and sugar. Our dough is a play on the latter type, though instead of sugar we use honey, and we also add some beer to our yeast mixture.

Olive oil and honey play important roles in the final taste of the crust. While I picked up this technique while working for chef Wolfgang Puck, it's widely used by many other pizza makers, particularly in the States. The addition of oil lowers the total amount of gluten formed and allows for a more tender crust, though it takes longer to bake than a traditional Neapolitan crust. Honey, which is essentially sugar, helps the crust to brown more evenly at a lower temperature. Without it, the crust would be paler and not as flavorful.

There are other factors that will improve your pizza game, such as hydration and the duration of fermentation. In regard to hydration, the dough should be wet and sticky—so sticky and wet, in fact, that you might start thinking to yourself that maybe it's a touch *too* wet. If the dough feels a little too compliant and too easy to work with, it's not wet enough. Wetter dough gives you lighter,

less dense pizza in the end, and should produce light, puffy air pockets around the edges. Certainly, when you're shaping the dough to make your pie, you can add more flour to prevent sticking, but while you're letting it rise, a properly hydrated dough is your best bet for delicious pizza crust down the road.

The fermentation time is also important. Letting the second rise happen slowly in a cold environment allows the dough to develop more complex taste. Ideally, you'd make the dough the day before baking and let it slowly rise in your refrigerator, but of course, sometimes planning ahead can be tricky, so making the dough in the morning to use that evening is OK, as well.

You can also easily double this recipe and have individually wrapped pizza dough balls at the ready in the freezer for whenever a pizza craving strikes. They defrost overnight in the refrigerator, and even faster at room temperature.

The pizza dough we share with you (see page 31) is an immensely flexible recipe, adaptable to becoming much more than just a vehicle for pizza toppings. You can use it to make focaccia (see page 147), pita (see page 201), and zeppole (see page 206). Mastering just one recipe will open doors to many uses. With time and muscle memory, you'll get the hang of it.

Tips for making pizza dough

It is far more preferable to work with sticky dough. Sticky dough means a wetter dough, and wetter dough means better-tasting pizza crust. However, sticky dough, well, sticks to everything, so can be tricky to work with. If you wet your hands and/or tools, the dough won't stick to them.

Weighing your ingredients is far more preferable to measuring by volume. The latter will almost always require you to adjust your dough one way or another, because everyone measures differently with cups and spoons, whereas weighing ingredients yields precise results each and every time.

A good way to see if you've kneaded your dough enough is the windowpane test: Take a small piece of dough off the mass, and gently stretch it out until it is paper-thin and translucent. If the dough tears before you can do this, your dough needs to be kneaded more.

Don't let your dough rise in the refrigerator too long. A few days' rise is fine and will enhance the taste of the crust, but any more than 3 days, and the yeast will start to eat up all the sugar in the dough and convert it into alcohol, which will adversely affect crust flavor.

An ideal fermentation window is 24 to 48 hours, but if you need to prepare pizza dough in the morning and make pizza that very night, that's OK, too.

In the recipes, I recommend that you make your pizza 12 inches (30.5 cm) wide, but if you're finding it difficult to stretch the dough out to that radius, don't worry about it. Just be sure to adjust the toppings slightly and put less on your pizza. Likewise, if you're getting an amoeba-shaped dough rather than a perfect circle, it's OK—just enjoy the rustic look of your pizza. It will still taste great!

PIZZA DOUGH

MAKES ENOUGH FOR 4 (12-INCH/30.5-CM) PIZZAS

We've spent quite a few years perfecting our pizza dough, and this is the version we finally felt achieved everything we wanted from our crust. This is our interpretation of a New York–style dough, which differs from its Neapolitan cousin by the addition of sugar and oil. In our version, beer imparts a delicate malted note, and the honey lends a touch of sweetness while aiding the browning process. Whole-wheat flour provides the dough with some heft as well as an earthy quality, and a little olive oil softens the glutens, making the bite more tender. The resulting crust is chewy but light, too, making for a pizza-eating experience that doesn't weigh you down.

½	cup (120 ml) beer, such as lager or pilsner, at room temperature (see Notes)
2	tablespoons mild honey
1	(¼-ounce/7-g) packet active dry yeast
3	cups plus 6 tablespoons (455 g) bread flour, plus more for stretching the dough
⅓	cup (40 g) whole-wheat flour
1	tablespoon kosher salt
2	tablespoons extra-virgin olive oil, plus more for oiling the bowl

In a small bowl, combine the beer and honey with 1 cup (240 ml) room temperature water. Sprinkle the yeast over the liquid and stir gently to dissolve. Let the mixture stand until it starts to foam, 5 to 10 minutes.

In a stand mixer fitted with a dough hook, combine the bread and whole-wheat flours and the salt. With the mixer running on low speed, add the oil, then the yeast mixture, increase the mixer speed to medium, and mix until the dough comes cleanly away from the sides of the bowl, 3 to 5 minutes.

Turn the dough out onto a clean work surface and knead by hand for 1 to 2 minutes. The dough should be pretty sticky; it should stick to your hands and the counter and leave behind a sticky trail. (If you think the dough is a bit too wet, it is probably just perfect. See Notes.) Gather the dough into a ball and place it in a lightly oiled bowl; turn it over to coat it with the oil. Cover the dough with a clean, damp towel and let it rise in a warm spot until doubled in size, about 30 minutes.

Gently punch down the dough, cover it with plastic wrap, and let it rise again in the refrigerator overnight or for up to 48 hours.

THE BASICS

31

Turn the dough out of the bowl onto a clean, lightly floured counter and knead gently for a few minutes. You will know when you have kneaded the dough enough when it passes the "windowpane test"—take a small piece of dough off the mass, and gently stretch it out until it is paper-thin and translucent. If your dough tears before you can do this, your dough needs to be kneaded more. Divide the dough into four equal balls, about 8 ounces (225 g) each—the size of large tangerines. Roll each ball under the palm of your hand until the top of the dough is smooth and firm. Pinch the bottom of the ball to seal the seam. If not using the dough immediately, wrap the dough balls individually in plastic wrap and freeze for up to two weeks. To thaw, transfer to the refrigerator one day before use or leave on the counter at room temperature for a couple of hours. If using right away, lightly dust the dough with flour and cover it with plastic wrap to prevent the dough from drying out. Let the dough come to room temperature for about 1 hour before making your pizza.

Before baking the pizza, be sure to preheat the oven to 500°F (260°C) and warm the pizza stone in it for at least 30 minutes.

———

Notes: When you are pouring the beer into the measuring cup, it will foam a great deal, so let the foam subside before adding more liquid to get to the right volume. If the dough is too wet, add a bit of flour, 1 tablespoon at a time. If the dough is too dry, try adding water, 1 tablespoon at a time, until you get to the right consistency. It may be hard to know at first if your dough is the perfect consistency, but you'll figure this out within making it just a handful of times.

HOW TO SHAPE THE DOUGH AND GET YOUR PIZZA IN THE OVEN

After you have made your dough according to the instructions on pages 31–33, allow it to come to room temperature for about 1 hour before making your pizza. Also be sure to preheat the oven to 500°F (260°C) and warm the pizza stone in it to at least 30 minutes.

Dip the dough into a little flour, shaking off the excess, and set on a clean, lightly floured counter.

Start stretching the dough with your hands, turning the ball as you press down the center.

Using your fingertips, dimple the dough a few times. Take it up in your hands, turning it with your fists, slowly pulling with each rotation to stretch.

Alternatively, if you find stretching by hand difficult, use a rolling pin to work the dough until you form a 12-inch (30.5-cm) circle.

It's okay if a hole or two forms. You can patch them by gently pulling some of the surrounding dough over to close and seal the tears.

Dust a wooden pizza peel with flour (if you don't have a peel, use an upside-down baking sheet generously dusted with flour) and slide it in under the dough.

Top your pizza according to the instructions of the recipe you're making or see pages 64-69 for guidance.

Slide the prepared pizza onto the hot pizza stone or baking sheet and bake until the crust is properly browned, about 10 minutes. Check the bottom of the pizza to make sure it has been cooked well—it should be rich brown and burnished.

Transfer the pizza to a cutting board. Do not cut the pie on your peel or you may damage it. Garnish as necessary, according to the recipe instructions, and cut into slices. Serve immediately.

RYE PIZZA DOUGH

MAKES ENOUGH FOR 4 (12-INCH/30.5-CM) PIZZAS

We originally developed this dough recipe to go with our Pastrami on Rye pizza (page 133), but truth be told, it's a great all-around dough to use whenever you feel like you want to use a bolder-tasting crust to go with a "heavier" type of pizza—think meat flavors such as ham, Meatballs (page 138), soppressata (see page 129), or Slow-Roasted Short Ribs (page 197), to name a few. We swap out honey and replace it with molasses for a deeper flavor to complement the rye flour, which has a more robust taste than whole wheat.

½	cup (120 ml) lager or other light-style beer (See Notes)
2	tablespoons unsulfured molasses
1	(¼-ounce/7-g) packet active dry yeast
3	cups plus 6 tablespoons (455 g) bread flour, plus more for stretching the dough
⅓	cup (45 g) dark rye flour
1	tablespoon kosher salt
2	tablespoons extra-virgin olive oil, plus more for oiling the bowl

In a small bowl, combine the beer and molasses with 1 cup (240 ml) room temperature water. Sprinkle the yeast over the liquid and stir gently to dissolve. Let the mixture stand until it starts to foam, 5 to 10 minutes.

In a stand mixer fitted with a dough hook, combine the bread and rye flours and the salt. With the mixer running on low speed, add the oil, then the yeast mixture, and mix until the dough comes cleanly away from the sides of the bowl, 3 to 5 minutes.

Turn the dough out onto a clean work surface and knead by hand for 1 to 2 minutes. The dough should be pretty sticky; it should stick to your hands and the counter and leave behind a sticky trail. (If you think the dough is a bit too wet, it is probably just perfect.) Gather the dough into a ball and place it in a lightly oiled bowl; turn it over to coat it with the oil. Cover the dough with a clean, damp towel and let it rise in a warm spot until doubled in size, about 30 minutes.

Gently punch down the dough, cover with plastic wrap, and let it rise in the refrigerator overnight or for up to 48 hours.

Turn the dough out of the bowl onto a clean, unfloured work surface and knead gently for a few minutes. You will know when you have kneaded the dough enough when it passes the "windowpane test"—take a small piece of dough off the mass and gently stretch it out until it is paper-thin and translucent. If your dough tears before you can do this, your dough needs to be kneaded more. Divide the dough into four equal balls, about 8 ounces (225 g) each—the size of large tangerines. Roll each ball under the palm of your hand until the top of the dough is smooth and firm. If not using the dough immediately, wrap the dough balls individually in plastic wrap and freeze for up to 2 weeks. To thaw, place in the refrigerator the night before or defrost at room temperature for about 2 hours. If using right away, cover it with a damp towel to prevent the dough from drying out. Let it come to room temperature for about 1 hour before making your pizza.

Before baking the pizza, be sure to preheat the oven to 500°F (260°C) and warm the pizza stone in it for at least 30 minutes.

———

Notes: When you are pouring the beer into the measuring cup, it will foam a great deal, so let the foam subside before adding more liquid to get to the right volume. If the dough is too wet, add a bit of flour, 1 tablespoon at a time. If the dough is too dry, try adding water, 1 tablespoon at a time, until you get to the right consistency. It may be hard to know at first if your dough is the perfect consistency, but you'll figure this out within making it just a handful of times.

GLUTEN-FREE PIZZA DOUGH

MAKES ENOUGH FOR 4 (12-INCH/30.5-CM) PIZZAS

While I'm immensely proud of our pizza dough (see page 31), I wanted to make sure that our patrons with gluten intolerance were also able to enjoy their pizza when dining at our restaurants. After playing around with various gluten-free versions, we settled on this one. It makes for a delicious pizza and produces a satisfying, chewy crust that doesn't feel like you are giving anything up. The addition of olive oil and honey provides flavor, as well as moisture, to the dough, and helps with the browning process, and xanthan gum, a naturally derived thickener from corn, replicates the chewy texture usually created by gluten, which is absent in this dough. It will feel a bit looser and more liquid than the gluten versions of our dough, so don't be alarmed if the consistency is different.

6	cups (896 g) gluten-free flour mix (we like King Arthur or Caputo's blends)
½	cup (63 g) dry milk powder
1	tablespoon plus 1 teaspoon baking powder
1	tablespoon plus 1 teaspoon xanthan gum
1	tablespoon kosher salt
1	quart (960 ml) warm water
¼	cup (60 ml) honey
10	tablespoons (150 ml) extra-virgin olive oil
2	tablespoons instant yeast

In a stand mixer fitted with a dough hook, combine the flour mix, milk powder, baking powder, xanthan gum, and salt. Mix on low speed until the dry ingredients are thoroughly blended.

In a small bowl, combine the water, honey, 2 tablespoons of the oil, the yeast, and about 2 cups (300 g) of the dry mixture; a few lumps are fine. Set the mixture aside for about 30 minutes, until the mixture is bubbly and smells yeasty.

Add this mixture to the remaining dry ingredients, and beat on medium-high speed for about 4 minutes. The mixture will be thick and sticky, like spackling compound. Cover the bowl with a clean, damp towel, and let the dough rest for about 30 minutes.

When ready to bake, preheat the oven to 425°F (220°C).

Drizzle 2 tablespoons of the oil onto the center of a baking sheet or a round pizza pan (see Note below). Scrape a quarter of the dough from the bowl onto the puddle of oil.

Using wet fingers, start at the center of the dough and work outward, pressing it into a 12-inch (30.5-cm) circle. Let the dough rest, uncovered, for 15 minutes. Keep in mind, the dough will spread when you bake it, so your pizza crust will wind up relatively thin. Repeat with the remaining oil and remaining three quarters of dough.

Bake the crust for 8 to 10 minutes, just until it's set; the surface will look opaque rather than shiny.

Remove from the oven and arrange your desired toppings. Return to the oven to finish baking, 10 to 15 minutes depending on the toppings, until the crust is baked through. Remove from the oven, cut into slices, and serve immediately.

Note: You could use a pizza stone, instead of a baking sheet or pizza pan, if you prefer. The results are the same. Warm the stone at 425°F (220°C) for at least 30 minutes before baking. Drizzle 2 tablespoons of the oil onto the center of a half-sheet piece of parchment paper, and scrape a quarter of the dough from the bowl onto the oil and paper. With wet fingers, press the dough into a 12-inch (30.5 cm) circle, starting at the center and working outward. Let the dough rest, uncovered, for 15 minutes. Place the crust (on the parchment) onto the stone, and bake it for 8 to 10 minutes, until just set. Remove the dough and stone from the oven and add the desired toppings. Return the pizza to the oven for another 10 to 15 minutes, until the toppings are cooked to the desired doneness.

SAUCES

Depending on the type of pizza you make, the best sauce to add will vary. While I provide you with sauce recommendations for each recipe here, as you get more into pizza making, you may choose to experiment with switching things up. My one piece of advice when it comes to sauce is that less is more (which applies to toppings, and everything, really, in my book, too). You can always make a second pizza and add more sauce if you decide you'd like to have more, but start with a modest amount, and even if you think the pizza is looking sparse, you're probably on the right track.

TOMATO SAUCE

MAKES ABOUT 3¼ CUPS (780 ML)

It should go without saying, but a good-tasting tomato will produce a superior sauce and, in turn, a superior pizza. As you see below, our tomato sauce couldn't be simpler. So, because it has just four ingredients, it's really all about the tomato. To find the perfect canned tomatoes, we did a blind taste test, trying about fifteen different varieties, from the most expensive San Marzanos to the cheapest supermarket brands. We were looking for balance: not super acidic, but also not flat. The perfect tomato for us wound up being from a company that sells tomatoes in giant cans to restaurants but not to home cooks. For the home kitchen, we think Muir Glen makes a delicious tomato and it is widely available, but follow your palate to find the one you like best. I recommend buying a few brands and tasting them side by side to find the one you really like. And when you find the perfect tomato, just mill it and add a little olive oil, salt, and pepper.

1	(28-ounce/793-g) can whole canned tomatoes
1	teaspoon kosher salt, plus more as needed
¼	teaspoon freshly ground black pepper
1	tablespoon extra-virgin olive oil

Using an immersion blender in a nonreactive container, or using a standing blender, puree the tomatoes for about 1 minute or until smooth. If using a standing blender, transfer the tomatoes to a nonreactive container. Add the salt, pepper, and oil, and whisk—do not blend—to combine. You want to whisk, because you are trying to just incorporate the oil into the sauce, whereas blending will aerate the sauce and also lighten its color, which we don't want to do.

Set aside until needed, or if not using right away, cover and refrigerate for up to 1 week or freeze up to 3 months.

MARINARA

Everyone needs a great, straightforward marinara recipe in his or her repertoire. Ours is flavored with some onions, garlic, salt, pepper, and basil, and given time to thicken. An important note to keep in mind when making this sauce (and other tomato sauces): Always simmer them uncovered to allow for moisture evaporation.

	Extra-virgin olive oil
2	medium yellow onions, diced
2	(28-ounce/793-g) cans whole tomatoes
1	large garlic clove, chopped
2	teaspoons kosher salt, or to taste
¼	teaspoon freshly ground black pepper, plus more as needed
¼	cup (10 g) basil leaves, roughly chopped

In a large heavy-bottomed ovenproof pot (such as a Dutch oven), add enough oil to cover the bottom of the pan, and warm the oil over medium heat until shimmering. Add the onions and cook, stirring, until translucent, about 5 minutes. Do not let the onions put on color.

Crush the tomatoes with your hands, and reserve the juices in the can. Add the garlic and tomatoes, pressing down on any large tomato chunks using a wooden spoon. Stir to combine, and bring to a simmer. Reduce the heat to maintain a simmer and cook, uncovered, until the sauce has thickened, 40 to 50 minutes. Season with the salt and pepper, and stir in the basil. Cook until the basil has sufficiently wilted, about 15 minutes.

Set aside in the pot until needed, or if not using right away, transfer to a container with a lid and refrigerate for up to 1 week or freeze for up to 3 months.

THE BASICS

45

PESTO

More of a spread than a sauce, this is thicker than what you normally think of when you think of pesto—and that's because it was mainly designed to go on pizza. If you have leftover pesto and would like to use it elsewhere (such as tossing with pasta), loosen it up with some olive oil to get the consistency you like.

2	large garlic cloves, peeled
1	tablespoon toasted pine nuts
2	cups (60 g) basil leaves
½	teaspoon kosher salt
	Pinch freshly ground black pepper
1	cup (240 ml) extra-virgin olive oil, plus more as needed
¾	cup (70 g) finely grated Parmigiano-Reggiano cheese

In a container with tall sides (a 1-quart/1-L deli container works great for this), layer the garlic, pine nuts, basil, salt, pepper, and oil—in that order. Using an immersion blender, blend until mostly emulsified and the basil leaves are tiny flecks, about 2 minutes. Fold in the cheese, cover, and refrigerate until needed, for up to 5 days. To prevent discoloration, store the pesto under a layer of olive oil.

THE BASICS

47

BÉCHAMEL

MAKES ABOUT 1 CUP (240 ML)

One of the "mother" sauces, aka, a sauce you will need to know how to make if you cook professionally, béchamel, simply put, is a slurry of butter, flour, and milk that is cooked until thickened. Master it and you're on your way to making a decent lasagna, or you have the base for a croque monsieur. We also like to use it on our pizza (see page 134).

2 tablespoons (30 g) unsalted butter

2 tablespoons all-purpose flour

1¼ cups (300 ml) whole milk, heated to hot

Kosher salt

Freshly ground black pepper

In a heavy-bottomed saucepan, melt the butter over medium heat until foaming. Stir in the flour and cook, stirring constantly, until a paste comes together and starts to bubble a bit, but don't let it brown—about 2 minutes. Pour in the heated milk, continuing to stir as the sauce thickens. Bring the liquid to a boil, and season to taste with salt and pepper. Decrease the heat to low, and cook for 2 to 3 minutes, stirring constantly, until the sauce is thick but still fairly liquid; it will continue to thicken as it cools.

Remove from the heat and transfer to a container with tall sides (a 1-quart/ 1-L deli container works great for this). Using an immersion blender, blend the béchamel until silky smooth. If not using right away, transfer to a jar and place a piece of wax paper over the surface of the sauce; this will prevent a skin from forming. Cover and refrigerate for up to 5 days.

PORCINI CREMA

MAKES ABOUT 1 CUP (240 ML)

When developing our mushroom pizza recipe (see page 80), we were looking for the best way to layer flavor to create the maximum level of umami. It was about concentrating as much of that mushroom taste as possible. Porcini, while expensive, are worth the splurge. A little goes a long way. Leftover porcini crema is delicious on pasta, so I suggest you make extra.

2	tablespoons (30 g) unsalted butter
1	small yellow onion, chopped
4	garlic cloves, chopped
3	thyme sprigs, leaves picked
½	bay leaf
¾	teaspoon kosher salt
⅛	teaspoon freshly ground black pepper
¼	cup (60 ml) white wine
¾	cup plus 2 tablespoons (210 ml) heavy cream
1	ounce (30 g) dried porcini mushrooms

In a medium saucepan, melt the butter over medium-high heat until foaming. Add the onion and garlic and cook, stirring, until translucent and fragrant, about 4 minutes. Do not let the vegetables put on color.

Reduce the heat to medium, and add the thyme leaves, bay leaf, salt, and pepper. Cook, stirring, until fragrant, about 1 minute.

Add the wine and cook, stirring, until the liquid is reduced by half, about 3 minutes. Add ¾ cup (180 ml) of the cream and the mushrooms, and bring to a simmer. Reduce the heat to low to maintain a gentle simmer, cover the saucepan, and cook, stirring from time to time, until the mushrooms are tender and the cream is the color of *dulce de leche*, about 10 minutes.

Remove from the heat, discard the bay leaf, and transfer the mixture to a 1-quart (1-L) deli container. Using an immersion blender, blend until completely smooth, being careful not to splash the hot liquid on yourself. The resulting porcini crema should have the consistency of yogurt. If the cream feels too stiff still, add the remaining 2 tablespoons cream and stir in with a fork until fully incorporated.

Let the cream cool to room temperature before using, or cover and refrigerate for up to 5 days.

ROSEMARY CREMA

Rosemary crema is my Italian answer to ranch dressing, and the perfect counterpoint to my Oven-Roasted Chicken Wings with Agrodolce Glaze (page 141). When we developed the recipe, we quickly discovered this sauce's hidden possibilities besides just being a dip: Use it as a base for pizza (see page 97), or toss with pasta for a quick, satisfying dinner.

½	cup (120 ml) My Favorite Mayonnaise (page 53) or store-bought
¼	cup (60 ml) well-shaken buttermilk
½	teaspoon fresh lemon juice
½	teaspoon finely chopped rosemary leaves
⅛	teaspoon onion powder
⅛	teaspoon garlic powder
⅛	teaspoon kosher salt, plus more as needed
	Small pinch freshly ground black pepper

In a container with tall sides (a 1-quart/1-L deli container works great for this), combine the mayonnaise, buttermilk, lemon juice, rosemary, onion and garlic powders, salt, and pepper. Using an immersion blender, blend until thoroughly emulsified. The rosemary bits will look like tiny confetti. Use immediately, or cover and refrigerate for up to 5 days.

PECORINO CREMA

MAKES ABOUT 1 QUART (1 LITER)

Rich and creamy, with a salty punch of Pecorino-Romano, this sauce is a perfect base for our Prosciutto Cotto Pizza (page 122), and is also excellent on any pizza when you're feeling a little decadent. Try it with roasted pumpkin (see page 97) or bitter greens (see page 134).

2	teaspoons extra-virgin olive oil
½	tablespoon (7 g) unsalted butter
½	yellow onion, diced
2	garlic cloves, smashed
3	thyme sprigs
½	cup (120 ml) white wine
1	cup (240 ml) whole milk
1	cup (240 ml) heavy cream
1	cup (100 g) finely grated Parmigiano-Reggiano cheese
1	cup (100 g) finely grated Pecorino-Romano cheese

In a small pan, warm the oil and butter over medium heat. Add the onion and garlic and cook, stirring, until the onion softens and is translucent, about 5 minutes. Add the thyme and stir until the mixture is aromatic, about 1 minute. Add the wine and cook until it almost evaporates, about 4 minutes.

Remove the mixture from the heat and transfer to a container with tall sides (a 1-quart/1-L deli container works great for this). Add the milk, cream, Parmigiano, and Pecorino. Using an immersion blender, process the mixture until smooth. Use immediately, or cover and refrigerate for up to 5 days.

MY FAVORITE MAYONNAISE

MAKES 3 CUPS (720 ML)

My mayonnaise recipe is unlike any others you've tried, and I am pretty confident it will become your favorite. I use whole soft-boiled eggs—yolks *and* whites—for the creamiest, richest, most delicious mayo. I find that using an immersion blender simplifies life quite a bit and makes for easy cleanup.

2	teaspoons kosher salt
3	large eggs
	Ice, for ice bath
1½	tablespoons Dijon mustard
2	cups (480 ml) canola or another neutral oil

Fill a medium pot with enough water to cover the eggs plus an additional 1 inch (2.5 cm). Add 1 teaspoon of the salt and bring the water to a boil. (Adding the salt will make peeling the eggs easier once they have been cooked.)

Meanwhile, in a large bowl, prepare an ice bath.

Gently lower the eggs into the boiling water and simmer for 4 minutes. Using a spider, transfer the eggs to an ice bath to immediately stop the cooking process. Let the eggs cool completely.

Crack the eggs on the counter and empty them into a large container with tall sides (a large 2-quart/2-L jar works great for this). Add the mustard and the remaining 1 teaspoon salt. Using an immersion blender, pulse the eggs until broken up, and with the motor running, slowly drizzle in the oil in a thin, steady stream until the mayonnaise is thick and creamy. Transfer to a clean jar and use immediately, or cover and refrigerate for up to 1 week.

ACCENTS

You're probably thinking, "What the hell are accents?" Accents are elements on a pizza that I can't quite classify as toppings or garnishes. Throughout the pizza recipe section (see pages 72–134), you'll see many toppings, garnishes, finishes, and so on, but the following few recipes are used prominently throughout the book. Regardless of what you call them, they're delicious.

GRILLED RED ONION

MAKES 1 ONION

At Genuine Pizza, we grill red onions until they're tender and browned, but for your home kitchen, you can choose to roast them in the oven with as much success (see Variation). These make a great addition to pizzas (see pages 107, 117) or salads (see page 172) and even work as a side to roasted chicken (see page 181).

1	medium red onion, peeled and sliced into rounds
	Extra-virgin olive oil
	Kosher salt
	Freshly ground black pepper

Preheat the grill (high heat for charcoal and medium for gas) or preheat a grill pan on medium.

Place the onions on a baking sheet and coat them with oil, then season with salt and pepper.

If using a charcoal grill: Arrange the onions on the opposite side of the grill from the charcoal. Be sure to keep the onion wedges intact when grilling. Cover the grill and cook the onions for 5 minutes. Uncover, flip the onions, replace the cover, and cook for another 5 minutes, or until the wedges soften and have grill marks.

If using a gas grill: Arrange the onions on the grill. Be sure to keep the onion wedges intact when grilling. Cover and cook for 7 minutes. Uncover, flip the onions, cover again, and cook for another 7 minutes, or until the wedges soften and have grill marks.

If using a grill pan: Arrange the onions on the grill pan. Be sure to keep the onion wedges intact when grilling. Grill the onions for 7 minutes. Flip the onions and grill for another 7 minutes, or until the wedges soften and have grill marks.

Remove the onion from the heat and let it cool to room temperature. Use immediately or cover and refrigerate for up to 3 days.

———

Variation: If you'd rather not grill, you can prepare this in your oven. Preheat the oven to 400°F (205°C). Place the onion on a baking sheet and coat with some oil, then season with salt and pepper. Be sure to keep the onion wedges intact when roasting. Place the onion in the oven and roast for 20 to 25 minutes, until tender and browned; do not stir. Remove from the oven and let it cool to room temperature. Use immediately or cover and refrigerate for up to 3 days.

CALABRIAN CHILE SAUCE

MAKES ABOUT 1 CUP (240 ML)

Calabrian chiles are worth seeking out either online or at a specialty shop (see page 236); they will add warm, measured heat to any dish, such as dressing (see page 176), pizza sauces (see pages 111, 113, 129), pimento cheese (see page 104), soup (see page 162), or even a michelada (see page 226), just to name a few. A small batch will last you awhile, and the sauce keeps fine in the fridge for a few weeks.

- ¾ cup (180 ml) extra-virgin olive oil
- 5 garlic cloves, minced

  Kosher salt
- 2 tablespoons crushed Calabrian chiles in oil (see Sources, page 236)
- ¼ cup (15 g) sun-dried tomatoes
- 1 teaspoon crushed red pepper
- ⅛ teaspoon freshly ground black pepper, plus more as needed
- 2 tablespoons red wine vinegar

In a heavy-bottomed pot, warm 6 tablespoons (90 ml) of the oil over medium heat until shimmering. Add the garlic and season with a pinch of salt. Cook, stirring, until the garlic is aromatic but does not put on color, 1 to 2 minutes. Add the chiles and tomatoes and cook, stirring, for about 1 minute. Add the crushed red pepper and black pepper and cook, stirring, until the spices are toasted, about 30 seconds. Add the vinegar, along with 2 tablespoons water, and bring the liquid to a boil.

    Remove from the heat, transfer to a container with tall sides (a 1-quart/1-L deli container works great for this) and add the remaining 6 tablespoons (90 ml) oil. Using an immersion blender, blend the sauce until completely emulsified. Taste and adjust salt and pepper, if needed. Transfer to a lidded jar and let cool completely before using. The sauce will keep, refrigerated, for 2 to 3 weeks.

CARAMELIZED ONIONS

MAKES ABOUT 1½ CUPS (465 G)

I want to file caramelized onions under the easiest, and yet hardest, things to make. The trick is simple: Take your time—you can't rush properly caramelized onions. Be prepared to cook them for at least one hour. Another trick for excellent results is to get a good sauté pan. I prefer a good heavy-bottomed stainless-steel pan or a Dutch oven such as Le Creuset, and not a cast-iron, to properly give the onions the time and opportunity to cook down. Cast-iron, while excellent at conducting heat, may burn the onions faster, and what you're looking for is slow caramelization. Because this takes so long, I recommend making as big a batch as your pan can handle and using the onions in various preparations, or freezing what you don't use. If you can get your hands on Vidalia onions, a sweet-tasting Southern seasonal favorite, I highly recommend it.

1½ teaspoons kosher salt, plus more as needed

2 tablespoons canola oil

1 tablespoon (15 g) unsalted butter

1½ pounds (680 g) yellow or Vidalia onions, peeled and thinly sliced

⅛ teaspoon freshly ground black pepper

Heat a large skillet on medium-low heat until hot. In a small bowl, measure out the salt and set aside. Add the oil and the butter to the skillet, and warm until the butter is melted. Add the onions and cook, stirring, for 4 minutes, until the onions start to become translucent. Season with a large pinch of salt from the bowl, and cook uncovered, stirring every few minutes to avoid scorching, for about 1 hour 30 minutes. As you are cooking the onions, occasionally season them with salt from the bowl.

When the onions are starting to turn brown, 15 to 20 minutes into the cooking, you can cover them with a piece of parchment paper cut into a circle (called a *cartouche*) to fit the inside of the pan. (This technique keeps just enough moisture in the onions to help them caramelize and not burn, but not so much moisture—as opposed to using a lid—that the onions steam instead.)

When the onions are fully caramelized, they will look dark brown and taste sweet. Season to taste with salt and pepper. Transfer to a covered container and let them cool. Use immediately, or cover and refrigerate for up to 1 week, or freeze for up to 3 months.

BRAISED FENNEL

MAKES ABOUT 3 CUPS (660 G; SEE NOTE)

This is another low-and-slow preparation that can be added to stews, soups, and of course (this being a pizza book) pizza. Mostly hands-off, the prep takes just a few minutes, and while the fennel is cooking, you can relax, cook something else, or make yourself a cocktail (see pages 220–226).

2	large fennel bulbs, trimmed and halved (or quartered if very large)
1½	cups (360 ml) low-sodium vegetable stock, plus more as needed
½	teaspoon kosher salt, plus more as needed
1	bay leaf

Preheat the oven to 325°F (165°C).

In an ovenproof dish, add the fennel and stock. The stock should come about one-quarter to one-third of the way up the sides of the fennel/dish. Add the salt and bay leaf. Cover the dish tightly with aluminum foil and transfer to the oven.

Braise the fennel until tender, about 1 hour and 15 minutes. Transfer to a cooling rack and let the fennel cool in the cooking liquid. Use immediately or transfer to a lidded container and refrigerate for up to 1 week.

Variation: If you don't have vegetable stock on hand, braise the fennel with ¾ cup (180 ml) water, ¾ cup (180 ml) extra-virgin olive oil, a couple of garlic cloves, a handful of fresh parsley, some salt, and a bay leaf. Save the resulting braising liquid to cook grains of your choosing—the broth will infuse them with more flavor.

Note: You're making more braised fennel than you need for a pizza. It is a delicious side dish drizzled with olive oil and sprinkled with Parmigiano-Reggiano shavings.

PRESERVED LEMONS

Preserved lemons are one of my favorite items to have on hand. This versatile pantry staple can be used any time you need lemons and would like to up the ante: roast chicken (see page 181), salad dressing, dips, pizza toppings—you name it. These lemons take mere minutes to prepare, and they will pay you back in spades in terms of flavor. If you're ever in a pinch, stores such as Whole Foods (or online retailers) carry ready-made preserved lemons, but making your own is much more rewarding—although it does require planning ahead by more than three weeks. One thing to keep in mind: It's very important to get organic lemons for preserving, as you will be using mostly the rind when the lemons are ready.

1 cup (240 g) kosher salt, plus more as needed

8 to 10 organic regular or Meyer lemons (about 2 pounds/910 kg)

Fresh lemon juice, as needed

Extra-virgin olive oil

Sterilize a 1-quart (1-L) jar. Place 1 tablespoon of the salt on the bottom.

Scrub the lemons thoroughly to make sure they are very clean and cut off any protruding stems from the fruit. Quarter the lemons and discard the seeds, then transfer the lemons to a large nonreactive bowl. Place the remaining salt in a second bowl nearby.

Put on a pair of clean disposable gloves—the salt can be pretty harsh on your hands. Place a layer of lemons in the jar and then generously sprinkle salt on top. Continue alternating lemons and salt until you run out of lemons.

Pack the lemons tightly in the jar, pressing down on them, so the extracted juices rise to the top of the jar. If the lemons do not produce enough juice, add more lemon juice as needed, until the jar is full. Cover, and let the jar sit at room temperature for 3 days.

Transfer the jar to the refrigerator and let it sit for at least 3 weeks. Every few days, turn the jar upside down.

After the 3 weeks have passed, drain and rinse the lemons. Dry them thoroughly, then pack them into a sterilized jar and cover them with oil. Be sure the lemons are fully submerged. To use, remove from the oil, pick out any remaining seeds, and utilize both the rind and flesh. The lemons will keep, refrigerated, for up to 6 months.

TOPPING YOUR PIE

There are no hard-and-fast rules on what makes a great-tasting pizza—the whole thing is completely subjective, as it all depends on what tastes good to you. However, as you contemplate pizzas you've liked, particularly your favorites, I bet you'll find some similarities. And as you're crafting your own pies at home, it is helpful to keep your favorite pizzas in mind for inspiration. You want the palate to be excited by what it tastes. For a pizza to be balanced, nuanced, and exciting, you need every bite to contain a variety of flavors and textures.

The possibilities for pizza toppings are endless but it can be hard to know where to start. So, to streamline the process and focus your approach, I have created a list of the key elements to consider when building a pizza.

Some pizzas shine best with many ingredients, and some may benefit from the singularity of a component. The simplified chart on the next page can help us map out how to make a pizza with varied, complementary flavors and textures.

ELEMENTS OF A PIZZA

Use this chart to start to map out your perfect pizza. You can select one of each, multiples, or even skip certain categories completely, but if you make an effort to select elements that fulfill different purposes on your pie, your topping combinations won't be one-note, overwhelming, or too subtle.

DOUGH	the other ingredients work together to accent this key element ↓ HERO TOPPING	SAUCE	CHEESE	one or two items that complement the hero ↓ SUPPORTING TOPPINGS	something green and fresh ↓ GARNISH	add a small amount right before serving ↓ FINISH
Regular	Spicy soppressata	Tomato	Mozzarella	Olives	Basil	Flaky salt
Gluten free	Anchovies	Pesto	Parmigiano-Reggiano	Pickled peppers	Arugula	Crushed red pepper
Rye	Shrimp	Puttanesca	Ricotta	Roasted lemon	Parsley	Drizzle of olive oil
	Mushrooms	Porcini crema	Fontina	Figs	Oregano	Freshly ground black pepper
	Meatballs	Caponata	Stracciatella	Honey		Sprinkling of Parmigiano
	Wilted greens	Béchamel		Peaches		
	Zucchini			Caramelized onions		
				Peppers and onions		

A pizza is greater than the sum of its parts. That's why supporting players, such as seasonings, garnishes, spices, and greens, are so important. They are the pixie dust, central to making pizza magic.

Of course, you can't just pick any topping and sauce combination and expect success. When you're working with several ingredients that have to share the same crust, you need to make sure they are all playing nicely together to make for a delicious pizza-eating experience.

Not to lead with the negative, but in some ways it's easier to suggest what might not work—as opposed to what will. The possibilities of flavor combinations are nearly limitless, but it might be a more effective tutorial to share what you may want to be cognizant of and skip.

For instance, I'd not pair puttanesca sauce—essentially marinara with olives, capers, and anchovies—with mushrooms, as that is too many strong flavors competing for your taste buds' attention. Nor would I pair rock shrimp with, say, rosemary crema (see page 51), as the bright marine taste of shrimp will be dulled by the rich and somewhat heavy cream sauce.

On the other hand, you may want to pair a rich, fatty ingredient such as roasted pork with something sweet (like figs) to cut through the richness. Or highlight briny, salty clams with the brightness of preserved lemon (or even regular lemon if no preserved lemon is on hand).

But, since your kitchen is your domain, I hope that in time you follow your intuition and create your own favorite combinations.

WINNING FLAVOR COMBINATIONS

Here are some of my favorite flavor combinations. I hope these lead you to discover some of the delicious recipes in this book and inspire you to create your own unique pizzas with the ingredients you have on hand and love, informed by these tried-and-true flavor profiles.

SALTY/BRINY
+
PUNCHY CHEESE
+
CITRUS
↓

Clams
+
Parmigiano-Reggiano
+
Pecorino-Romano
+
preserved lemon (page 121)

Rock shrimp
+
Manchego
+
roasted lemon
(page 89)

SALTY
+
RICH
+
CREAMY
↓

Bacon
+
Taleggio
(page 108)

Merguez
+
halloumi
(page 125)

Bacon
+
egg
+
cheese
(page 126)

Roasted okra
+
pimento cheese
(page 103)

Pastrami
+
buttermilk
+
mayonnaise
(page 133)

Prosciutto cotto
+
Pecorino crema
(page 122)

EARTHY/ NEUTRAL

+

CREAMY

Cremini
+
porcini crema
(page 80)

Zucchini
+
ricotta
(page 131)

Wilted greens
+
béchamel
(page 134)

Broccolini
+ Fontina
(page 113)

Pesto
+
ricotta
+
mozzarella
(page 93)

Roasted Pumpkin
+ Brussels sprouts
+ rosemary crema (page 97)

Creamed kale
+ caramelized
onions
+ Fontina
(page 94)

Braised fennel
+
Trugole
(page 114)

TOMATO- FORWARD

+

CREAMY

Puttanesca
+
stracciatella
(page 101)

Tomato sauce
+
mozzarella
(page 72)

Tomato sauce
+
Fontina
(page 75)

Caponata
+
mozzarella
(page 76)

Spicy roasted
tomato sauce
+
stracciatella
(page 111)

RICH/FATTY

+

GOOD MELTING CHEESE

+

SWEET

Slow-roasted pork
+ Fontina
+ figs (page 107)

Spicy soppressata
+ Fontina
+ mozzarella
+ honey (page 129)

Gorgonzola cheese
+ Fontina
+ peach (page 117)

Bacon
+ Fontina
+ Gruyère
+ caramelized
onions (page 83)

Taleggio
+ Fontina
+ figs (page 118)

Short rib
+ Gruyère
+ caramelized
onions (page 79)

Meatball
+ Trugole
+ peppers and
onions (page 85)

PUTTING IT
ALL TOGETHER

THE
PIZZA
RECIPES

PART II

MARGHERITA PIZZA

MAKES 1 (12-INCH/30.5-CM) PIZZA

A margherita pizza is a great place to start if you're new to making pizza, and for many, this is the benchmark by which all pizza is judged. And it's a crowd favorite for a reason. With so few ingredients, the margherita speaks to the art of simplicity. Here, less is truly more. Is the dough light, airy, and chewy? Are the ingredients carefully curated and are the proportions right? When looking for mozzarella, look for the fresh type that is not buffalo mozzarella, which tends to be too wet.

1   (8-ounce/225-g) ball Pizza Dough (page 31), at room temperature

Flour, for rolling

¼   cup (60 ml) Tomato Sauce (page 44)

1   cup (110 g) diced fresh mozzarella

Kosher salt

4   large basil leaves, torn

Extra-virgin olive oil, for garnishing

At least 30 minutes before baking, place a pizza stone or baking sheet on a baking rack in the top third of the oven, and preheat the oven to 500°F (260°C).

After you have made your dough according to the instructions on pages 31–35 allow the dough to come to room temperature for about 1 hour before making your pizza. Dip the dough into a little flour, shaking off the excess, and set on a clean, lightly floured counter. Start stretching the dough with your hands, turning the ball as you press down the center. Then, using either your hands or a rolling pin (if you're finding stretching the dough by hand to be tricky), work the dough until you form a 12-inch (30.5-cm) circle. If any holes form in the dough, patch them up so the topping does not seep through.

Dust a wooden pizza peel with flour (if you don't have a peel, use an upside-down baking sheet generously dusted with flour) and slide it in under the dough.

Using the back of a large spoon, and starting from the center and spiraling your way out, distribute the tomato sauce in a thin, even layer. You want to see some of the dough peeking through. Sprinkle the mozzarella on top and season with a pinch of salt.

Slide the prepared pizza onto the hot pizza stone or baking sheet and bake until the crust is properly browned, about 10 minutes. Check the bottom of the pizza to make sure it has been cooked well—it should be rich brown and burnished. Transfer the pizza to a cutting board, garnish with the basil and oil, and cut into slices. Serve immediately.

CLASSIC CHEESE PIZZA

MAKES 1 (12-INCH/30.5-CM) PIZZA

This pizza came out of our attempt to satisfy kids who just wanted plain cheese pizza, and viewed the Margherita (page 72) with suspicion and wouldn't eat it. The white blobs of melted mozzarella, plus all that basil, seemed too weird. So, we created something closer to a traditional cheese pizza, but packed with more flavor than something you'd get at a corner pizzeria. I like to turn up the heat with some crushed red pepper and sometimes even a little Calabrian Chile Sauce (page 57). The pizza was so popular, it became our second bestseller next to the Margherita.

1	(8-ounce/225-g) ball Pizza Dough (page 31), at room temperature
	Flour, for rolling
¼	cup (60 ml) Tomato Sauce (page 44)
	Scant ⅔ cup (2 ounces/57 g) coarsely grated Fontina cheese
	Kosher salt
2	tablespoons finely grated Parmigiano-Reggiano cheese
	Crushed red pepper flakes, for serving

At least 30 minutes before baking, place a pizza stone or baking sheet on a baking rack in the top third of the oven, and preheat the oven to 500°F (260°C).

After you have made your dough according to the instructions on pages 31–35, allow the dough to come to room temperature for about 1 hour before making your pizza. Dip the dough into a little flour, shaking off the excess, and set on a clean, lightly floured counter. Start stretching the dough with your hands, turning the ball as you press down the center. Then, using either your hands or a rolling pin (if you're finding stretching the dough by hand to be tricky), work the dough until you form a 12-inch (30.5-cm) circle. If any holes form in the dough, patch them up so the topping does not seep through.

Dust a wooden pizza peel with flour (if you don't have a peel, use an upside-down baking sheet generously dusted with flour) and slide it in under the dough.

Using the back of a large spoon, and starting from the center and spiraling your way out, distribute the tomato sauce in a thin, even layer. You want to see some of the dough peeking through. Sprinkle with the Fontina and a pinch of salt.

Slide the prepared pizza onto the hot pizza stone or baking sheet and bake until the crust is properly browned, about 10 minutes. Check the bottom of the pizza to make sure it has been cooked well—it should be rich brown and burnished. Transfer the pizza to a cutting board, garnish with the Parmigiano, and crushed red pepper and cut into slices. Serve immediately.

CAPONATA PIZZA

MAKES 1 (12-INCH/30.5-CM) PIZZA

I love eggplant, and one of my favorite ways to use it is to make caponata (see page 147). Served alongside some warm focaccia, caponata is a great way to kick off a meal. It's also a terrific pizza topping: Soft, sweet-and-sour eggplant, studded with plump raisins, pairs well with fresh mozzarella and salty Pecorino-Romano. Fresh basil, as a finishing touch, makes this a perfect pizza to make in the summer, when eggplant is at its best. And because I love using one dish in as many ways as possible, using leftover caponata on pizza helps you to be a little bit more efficient in the kitchen.

1	(8-ounce/225-g) ball Pizza Dough (page 31), at room temperature
	Flour, for rolling
¼	cup (60 ml) Caponata (page 147) or a quality store-bought eggplant-and-tomato spread
¼	cup (30 g) fresh salted mozzarella cheese, diced
2	tablespoons finely grated Pecorino-Romano cheese
6	basil leaves, torn

At least 30 minutes before baking, place a pizza stone or baking sheet on a baking rack in the top third of the oven, and preheat the oven to 500°F (260°C).

After you have made your dough according to the instructions on pages 31–35, allow the dough to come to room temperature for about 1 hour before making your pizza. Dip the dough into a little flour, shaking off the excess, and set on a clean, lightly floured counter. Start stretching the dough with your hands, turning the ball as you press down the center. Then, using either your hands or a rolling pin (if you're finding stretching the dough by hand to be tricky), work the dough until you form a 12-inch (30.5-cm) circle. If any holes form in the dough, patch them up so the topping does not seep through.

Dust a wooden pizza peel with flour (if you don't have a peel, use an upside-down baking sheet generously dusted with flour) and slide it in under the dough.

Spread the caponata on top, then add the mozzarella. Sprinkle with half of the Pecorino and top with the basil.

Slide the prepared pizza onto the hot pizza stone or baking sheet and bake until the crust is properly browned, about 10 minutes. Check the bottom of the pizza to make sure it has been cooked well—it should be rich brown and burnished. Transfer the pizza to a cutting board, garnish with the remaining Pecorino, and cut into slices. Serve immediately.

SHORT RIB PIZZA

WITH CARAMELIZED ONIONS, GRUYÈRE, AND ARUGULA MAKES 1 (12-INCH/30.5-CM) PIZZA

Every pizzeria worth its salt has its signature pizza, and this is ours. Roasting the short ribs just for the pizza is the wrong move—but make the short ribs for dinner, make extra, and save some for the pizza. It's damn good, and I dare you to make it and *not* like it.

1 (8-ounce/225-g) ball Pizza Dough (page 31), at room temperature

Flour, for rolling

¼ cup (25 g) coarsely grated Fontina cheese

¼ cup (25 g) coarsely grated Gruyère cheese

3 to 4 tablespoons Caramelized Onions (page 58)

½ cup (80 g) coarsely grated Slow-Roasted Short Ribs (page 193)

Kosher salt

¼ cup (5 g) arugula

At least 30 minutes before baking, place a pizza stone or baking sheet on a baking rack in the top third of the oven, and preheat the oven to 500°F (260°C).

After you have made your dough according to the instructions on pages 31–35, allow the dough to come to room temperature for about 1 hour before making your pizza. Dip the dough into a little flour, shaking off the excess, and set on a clean, lightly floured counter. Start stretching the dough with your hands, turning the ball as you press down the center. Then, using either your hands or a rolling pin (if you're finding stretching the dough by hand to be tricky), work the dough until you form a 12-inch (30.5-cm) circle. If any holes form in the dough, patch them up so the topping does not seep through.

Dust a wooden pizza peel with flour (if you don't have a peel, use an upside-down baking sheet generously dusted with flour) and slide it in under the dough.

Mix the Fontina and Gruyère in a small bowl until combined. Spread the cheese blend evenly on the pizza. Scatter the onions and meat over the cheese, and sprinkle with a pinch of salt.

Slide the prepared pizza onto the hot pizza stone or baking sheet and bake until the crust is properly browned, about 10 minutes. Check the bottom of the pizza to make sure it has been cooked well—it should be rich brown and burnished. Transfer the pizza to a cutting board, top with the arugula, and cut into slices. Serve immediately.

MUSHROOM PIZZA

MAKES 1 (12-INCH/30.5-CM) PIZZA

I love mushrooms, and when we were putting together our mushroom pizza, we wanted to make a pie that maximized the intense umami-rich mushrooms. We decided on a porcini-cream base (see page 49) to highlight and complement the cremini mushrooms, and added punchy Taleggio cheese, as it stands up well to strong mushroom flavor. The resulting pizza is one of my favorites.

1 (8-ounce/225-g) ball Pizza Dough (page 31), at room temperature

Flour, for rolling

2 tablespoons Porcini Crema (page 49), at room temperature

1 (1-ounce/30 g) piece Taleggio cheese (about the size of 2 unshelled walnuts), torn into pieces

Scant ⅔ cup (70 g) coarsely grated Fontina cheese

2 large cremini mushroom caps, thinly sliced

Kosher salt

Thyme leaves, for garnishing

At least 30 minutes before baking, place a pizza stone or baking sheet on a baking rack in the top third of the oven, and preheat the oven to 500°F (260°C).

After you have made your dough according to the instructions on pages 31–35, allow the dough to come to room temperature for about 1 hour before making your pizza. Dip the dough into a little flour, shaking off the excess, and set on a clean, lightly floured counter. Start stretching the dough with your hands, turning the ball as you press down the center. Then, using either your hands or a rolling pin (if you're finding stretching the dough by hand to be tricky), work the dough until you form a 12-inch (30.5-cm) circle. If any holes form in the dough, patch them up so the topping does not seep through.

Using the back of a large spoon, and starting from the center and spiraling your way out, distribute the porcini crema, in a thin, even layer. Add the Taleggio, Fontina, mushrooms, and salt.

Slide the prepared pizza onto the hot pizza stone or baking sheet and bake until the crust is properly browned, about 10 minutes. Check the bottom of the pizza to make sure it has been cooked well—it should be rich brown and burnished. Transfer the pizza to a cutting board, garnish with the thyme, and cut into slices. Serve immediately.

BACON AND POTATO PIZZA

MAKES 1 (12-INCH/30.5-CM) PIZZA

Pizza con patate is wildly popular in Rome, and for a while, potato pizza was a thing in the States as well. We loved the idea behind it, but were craving something slightly different. The resulting marriage of potatoes, cheese, and bacon, served with a heap of fresh arugula, is substantial but doesn't feel too heavy.

Extra-virgin olive oil

¼ cup (56 g) diced bacon

1 (8-ounce/225-g) ball Pizza Dough (page 31), at room temperature

Flour, for rolling

½ cup (55 g) coarsely grated Fontina cheese

½ cup (55 g) coarsely grated Gruyère cheese

2 tablespoons Caramelized Onions (page 58)

1 to 2 fingerling or creamer potatoes, blanched until fork-tender and cut into slices ¼ to ½ inch (6 to 12 mm) thick

1 teaspoon chopped rosemary leaves

Kosher salt

½ cup (10 g) arugula

At least 30 minutes before baking, place a pizza stone or baking sheet on a baking rack in the top third of the oven, and preheat the oven to 500°F (260°C).

Meanwhile, cook the bacon (see page 108).

After you have made your dough according to the instructions on pages 31–35 allow the dough to come to room temperature for about 1 hour before making your pizza. Dip the dough into a little flour, shaking off the excess, and set on a clean, lightly floured counter. Start stretching the dough with your hands, turning the ball as you press down the center. Then, using either your hands or a rolling pin (if you're finding stretching the dough by hand to be tricky), work the dough until you form a 12-inch (30.5-cm) circle. If any holes form in the dough, patch them up so the topping does not seep through.

Dust a wooden pizza peel with flour (if you don't have a peel, use an upside-down baking sheet generously dusted with flour) and slide it in under the dough.

Top the dough with the Fontina, Gruyère, onions, bacon, potatoes, and rosemary, and sprinkle with a pinch of salt. Slide the prepared pizza onto the hot pizza stone or baking sheet and bake until the crust is properly browned, about 10 minutes. Check the bottom of the pizza to make sure it has been cooked well—it should be rich brown and burnished. Transfer the pizza to a cutting board, garnish with the arugula, and cut into slices. Serve immediately.

MEATBALL PIZZA

MAKES 1 (12-INCH/30.5-CM) PIZZA

I'm a big fan of the "cook once, eat twice (or even three times)" philosophy. While this is how restaurants typically function—cross utilization of ingredients and preparations—I feel this approach is even more important for a home cook to master, as it will save you loads of time. This pizza is our homage to a more traditional combination of sausage, peppers, and onions. At the restaurant, we always have meatballs (see page 138), which are one of our most popular menu items. We use some of those meatballs on pizza—and we absolutely love the result. Obviously, don't make meatballs just to make the pizza; make meatballs because they are delicious, and because you'll be able to use them in pizza, as well. If, after making this pizza, you find yourself with extra meatballs and peppers and onions, you've got the makings of a delicious sub—just add Provolone cheese. A single effort will give you two—or even three— delicious meals—and what could be better than that? Extra escarole means you can make my favorite salad (see page 167).

1	(8-ounce/225-g) ball Pizza Dough (page 31), at room temperature
	Flour, for rolling
2	tablespoons Tomato Sauce (page 44)
	A generous ½ cup (55 g) coarsely grated Provolone cheese
2	tablespoons Peppers and Onions (recipe follows)
½	cup (30 g) chopped escarole
1	Meatball (page 138), crumbled
	Kosher salt

At least 30 minutes before baking, place a pizza stone or baking sheet on a baking rack in the top third of the oven, and preheat the oven to 500°F (260°C).

After you have made your dough according to the instructions on pages 31–35, allow the dough to come to room temperature for about 1 hour before making your pizza. Dip the dough into a little flour, shaking off the excess, and set on a clean, lightly floured counter. Start stretching the dough with your hands, turning the ball as you press down the center. Then, using either your hands or a rolling pin (if you're finding stretching the dough by hand to be tricky), work the dough until you

form a 12-inch (30.5-cm) circle. If any holes form in the dough, patch them up so the topping does not seep through.

Dust a wooden pizza peel with flour (if you don't have a peel, use an upside-down baking sheet generously dusted with flour) and slide it in under the dough.

Using the back of a large spoon, and starting from the center and spiraling your way out, distribute the tomato sauce in a thin, even layer. You want to see some of the dough peeking through. Scatter the cheese, peppers and onions, escarole, and meatball over the dough, then sprinkle with a pinch of salt.

Slide the prepared pizza onto the hot pizza stone or baking sheet and bake until the crust is properly browned, about 10 minutes. Check the bottom of the pizza to make sure it has been cooked well—it should be rich brown and burnished. Transfer the pizza to a cutting board and cut into slices. Serve immediately.

PEPPERS AND ONIONS

MAKES 1½ CUPS (150 G)

2	tablespoons extra-virgin olive oil
1	large yellow or Vidalia onion (8 ounces/225 g), peeled, halved, and thinly sliced
1	large red bell pepper (8 ounces/225 g), seeded and thinly sliced
1	teaspoon kosher salt
⅛	teaspoon freshly ground black pepper

In a large, heavy-bottomed pan, warm the oil over medium-high heat until shimmering. Add the onion and cook, stirring, until translucent and softened, about 4 minutes. Add the red bell pepper, reduce the heat to medium, and cook, stirring, until the pepper softens considerably, about 10 minutes. Reduce the heat to medium-low, add the salt and pepper, and cover. Cook, stirring from time to time, until the onion and pepper slices have collapsed and are about half of their precooked volume, about 1 hour. Use immediately, or cover and refrigerate for up to 1 week.

SHRIMP PIZZA

WITH ROASTED LEMON, SCALLION, AND CILANTRO MAKES 1 (12-INCH/30.5-CM) PIZZA

Putting seafood on pizza is always a gamble, and this pizza, when we put it on the menu, was a veritable dark horse. When we were toying with the idea of putting shrimp on pizza, we loved the flavors, but we weren't sure people were going to order a pizza with rock shrimp, scallions, and cilantro. (Who puts cilantro on a pizza?) I also wanted the tart, bright lemon note, and thought if I sliced the lemons thinly, roasted them, and then cooked them on pizza that they would be tasty—and I was right. Today this is one of our more popular pizzas, as it showcases rock shrimp, which is a favorite local Floridian ingredient. Because shrimp turn rubbery when overcooked, this is one of the pizzas you want to err on the side of undercooking ever so slightly. As for any extra roasted lemons, you can add them to salads, while roasting a chicken (see page 181) or fish, or any recipe that calls for regular lemon.

½ cup (85 g) shelled and deveined rock shrimp or other small shrimp

1 (8-ounce/225-g) ball Pizza Dough (page 31), at room temperature

Flour, for rolling

¼ cup (25 g) coarsely grated Manchego cheese

¼ cup (25 g) coarsely grated Fontina cheese

1 tablespoon finely chopped Roasted Lemon (recipe follows)

2 tablespoons scallions, thinly sliced on the bias

1 tablespoon whole cilantro leaves

Kosher salt, for garnishing

At least 30 minutes before baking, place a pizza stone or baking sheet on a baking rack in the top third of the oven, and preheat the oven to 500°F (260°C).

Meanwhile, place the rock shrimp between two pieces of paper towels and blot dry. Let sit while you prepare the pizza dough to ensure that the excess moisture gets absorbed.

After you have made your dough according to the instructions on pages 31–35, allow the dough to come to room temperature for about 1 hour before making your pizza. Dip the dough into a little flour, shaking off the excess, and set on a clean, lightly floured counter. Start stretching the dough with your hands, turning the ball as you press down the center. Then, using either your hands or a rolling pin (if you're finding stretching the dough by hand to be tricky), work the dough until you form a 12-inch (30.5-cm) circle. If any holes form in the dough, patch them up so the topping does not seep through.

Dust a wooden pizza peel with flour (if you don't have a peel, use an upside-down baking sheet generously dusted with flour) and slide it in under the dough.

Evenly scatter the Manchego, Fontina, lemon, and shrimp on top. Slide the prepared pizza onto the hot pizza stone or baking sheet and bake until the crust is properly browned, about 10 minutes. Check the bottom of the pizza to make sure it has been cooked well—it should be rich brown and burnished. Transfer the pizza to a cutting board, garnish with the scallions and cilantro, and sprinkle with salt to taste. Cut into slices and serve immediately.

ROASTED LEMON

MAKES ABOUT ¾ CUP (145 G)

2   lemons, quartered

Preheat the oven to 425°F (220°C).

Cut the lemon into quarters or sixths and trim the pieces so you're left with the rind, pith, and a thin layer of the pulp. Save the remaining lemon pulp for another use. Arrange the lemons in a single layer, cut side down, on a half-sheet baking pan (18 by 13 inches/46 by 33 cm) and roast in the oven until the lemon pieces start to char, about 10 minutes. Remove from the oven, let cool, and cut into ¼-inch (6-mm) dice. Transfer to a nonreactive container, cover, and refrigerate until needed. The roasted lemon will keep, refrigerated, for up to 1 week.

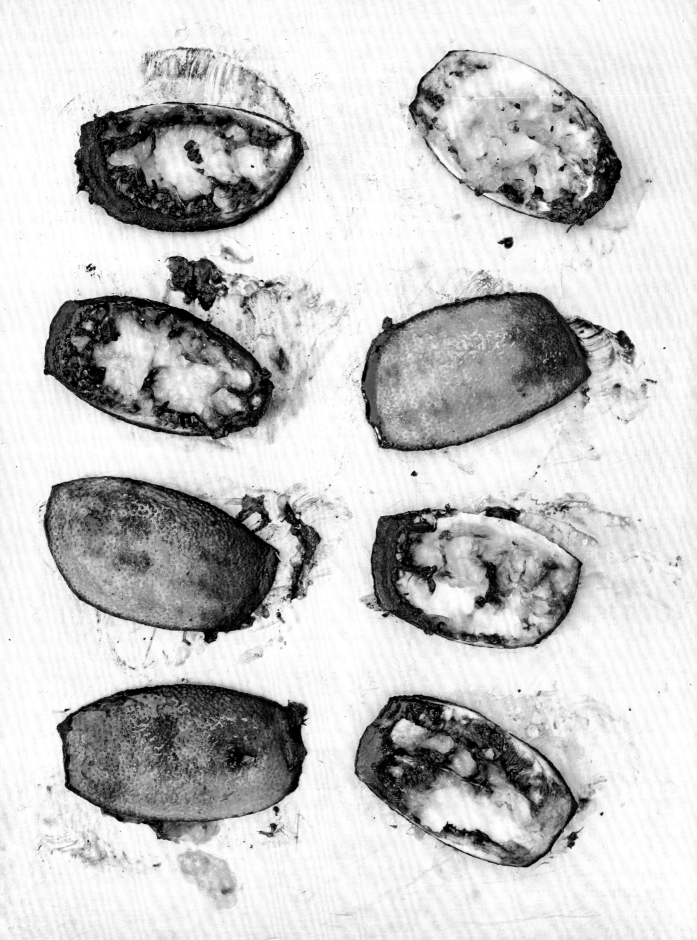

PESTO PIZZA

WITH FRESH TOMATO AND HOMEMADE RICOTTA   MAKES 1 (12-INCH/30.5-CM) PIZZA

When you use peak-season heirloom tomatoes, sliced so thin you can see light shine through them, plus fresh pesto, the flavors on this pizza just sing. Keep your pesto on the drier and stiffer (but still spreadable) side to prevent the pizza from getting overly oily. Loosen the remaining pesto with some oil and toss with pasta.

1   (8-ounce/225-g) ball Pizza Dough (page 31), at room temperature

Flour, for rolling

2   tablespoons Pesto (page 47) or store-bought

1   ounce (30 g) fresh mozzarella cheese, torn into small pieces

6   to 7 thin slices heirloom tomato

2   tablespoons Homemade Ricotta (page 150) or store-bought

Kosher salt

2   tablespoons finely grated Pecorino-Romano cheese

At least 30 minutes before baking, place a pizza stone or baking sheet on a baking rack in the top third of the oven, and preheat the oven to 500°F (260°C).

After you have made your dough according to the instructions on pages 31–35, allow the dough to come to room temperature for about 1 hour before making your pizza. Dip the dough into a little flour, shaking off the excess, and set on a clean, lightly floured counter. Start stretching the dough with your hands, turning the ball as you press down the center. Then, using either your hands or a rolling pin (if you're finding stretching the dough by hand to be tricky), work the dough until you form a 12-inch (30.5-cm) circle. If any holes form in the dough, patch them up so the topping does not seep through.

Dust a wooden pizza peel with flour (if you don't have a peel, use an upside-down baking sheet generously dusted with flour) and slide it in under the dough.

Using the back of a large spoon, and starting from the center and spiraling your way out, distribute the pesto. Top with the mozzarella, tomato, and dollops of ricotta, and a pinch of salt.

Slide the prepared pizza onto the hot pizza stone or baking sheet and bake until the crust is properly browned, about 10 minutes. Check the bottom of the pizza to make sure it has been cooked well—it should be rich brown and burnished. Transfer the pizza to a cutting board, garnish with the Pecorino, and cut into slices. Serve immediately.

KALE PIZZA

WITH CARAMELIZED ONION AND FONTINA
MAKES 1 (12-INCH/30.5-CM) PIZZA

We wanted to do a play on spinach-artichoke dip on pizza, and thought creamed kale would make a perfect sauce base, resulting in an indulgent pie. To break through the richness, and for a bit of heat, we add some crushed red pepper. As for the remaining creamed kale, which you'll have on hand, it goes great tossed with some pasta and topped with grated Parmigiano-Reggiano!

1	(8-ounce/225-g) ball Pizza Dough (page 31), at room temperature
	Flour, for rolling
2	tablespoons Creamed Kale (recipe follows)
¼	cup (25 g) coarsely grated Fontina cheese
2	tablespoons Caramelized Onions (page 58)
½	cup (35 g) chopped kale
¼	cup (25 g) finely grated Parmigiano-Reggiano cheese
	Crushed red pepper, for garnishing

At least 30 minutes before baking, place a pizza stone or baking sheet on a baking rack in the top third of the oven, and preheat the oven to 500°F (260°C).

After you have made your dough according to the instructions on pages 31–35, allow the dough to come to room temperature for about 1 hour before making your pizza. Dip the dough into a little flour, shaking off the excess, and set on a clean, lightly floured counter. Start stretching the dough with your hands, turning the ball as you press down the center. Then, using either your hands or a rolling pin (if you're finding stretching the dough by hand to be tricky), work the dough until you form a 12-inch (30.5-cm) circle. If any holes form in the dough, patch them up so the topping does not seep through.

Dust a wooden pizza peel with flour (if you don't have a peel, use an upside-down baking sheet generously dusted with flour) and slide it in under the dough.

Using the back of a large spoon, and starting from the center and spiraling your way out, distribute the creamed kale. Add the Fontina, onions, and kale.

Slide the prepared pizza onto the hot pizza stone or baking sheet and bake until the crust is properly browned, about 10 minutes. Check the bottom of the pizza to make sure it has been cooked well—it should be rich brown and burnished. Transfer the pizza to a cutting board, garnish with the Parmigiano and crushed red pepper, and cut into slices. Serve immediately.

CREAMED KALE

MAKES ABOUT 2¼ CUPS (600 G)

2	tablespoons (30 g) unsalted butter
1	small yellow onion, diced
1	large garlic clove, chopped
1	bay leaf
½	teaspoon kosher salt, plus more as needed
4	cups (260 g) chopped kale
¼	teaspoon freshly ground black pepper, plus more as needed
¼	teaspoon crushed red pepper, plus more as needed
¼	cup (60 ml) white wine
1	cup (240 ml) heavy cream

In a large skillet, melt the butter over low heat until it foams. Add the onion, garlic, and bay leaf, and cook, stirring, until the onion has softened, 4 to 5 minutes. Add the salt and stir to incorporate.

Add the kale, black pepper, and crushed red pepper and cook, stirring, until the kale starts to wilt, about 2 minutes. Add the wine and cook, stirring, until it has reduced by half, about 3 minutes. Add the cream and cook, stirring, until it has reduced by about a quarter, about 7 minutes. Discard the bay leaf, transfer the mixture to a container with tall sides (a 1-quart/1-L deli container works great for this). Using an immersion blender, process the mixture until smooth. Use immediately, or cover and refrigerate for up to 4 days. You can also freeze the creamed kale for up to 2 months.

ROASTED PUMPKIN PIZZA

WITH BRUSSELS SPROUTS AND ROSEMARY
CREMA MAKES 1 (12-INCH/30.5-CM) PIZZA

Calabaza, also known as West Indian pumpkin, is a winter squash popular in the Caribbean and tropical America. It's generally bright orange with mildly sweet, firm flesh. And it makes a terrific pizza topping, particularly as we start heading toward fall. This pizza is an excellent seasonal addition to our autumn menu. (Unfortunately calabaza season doesn't last long, and once it's gone, so is the pizza.) If you can't find calabaza, butternut squash makes for a fine substitute. Be sure to shave the squash into paper-thin ribbons (a Y-shaped vegetable peeler is your best asset here; see page 21) for a beautiful presentation and some delicious, crispy browned edges.

1	(8-ounce/225-g) ball Pizza Dough (page 31), at room temperature
	Flour, for rolling
¼	cup (60 ml) Rosemary Crema (page 51)
½	cup (55 g) coarsely grated Gruyère cheese
½	cup (55 g) coarsely grated Fontina cheese
1	cup (90 g) shaved paper-thin calabaza squash
2	tablespoons Caramelized Onions (page 58)
2	Brussels sprouts, leaves removed and separated
2	tablespoons finely grated Parmigiano-Reggiano

At least 30 minutes before baking, place a pizza stone or baking sheet on a baking rack in the top third of the oven, and preheat the oven to 500°F (260°C).

After you have made your dough according to the instructions on pages 31–35, allow the dough to come to room temperature for about 1 hour before making your pizza. Dip the dough into a little flour, shaking off the excess, and set on a clean, lightly floured counter. Start stretching the dough with your hands, turning the ball as you press down the center. Then, using either your hands or a rolling pin (if you're finding stretching the dough by hand to be tricky), work the dough until you form a 12-inch (30.5-cm) circle. If any holes form in the dough, patch them up so the topping does not seep through.

Dust a wooden pizza peel with flour (if you don't have a peel, use an upside-down baking sheet generously dusted with flour) and slide it in under the dough.

Using the back of a large spoon, and starting from the center and spiraling your way out, spread the crema. Add the Gruyère, Fontina, squash, onions, and Brussels sprout leaves.

Slide the prepared pizza onto the hot pizza stone or baking sheet and bake until the crust is properly browned, about 10 minutes. Check the bottom of the pizza to make sure it has been cooked well—it should be rich brown and burnished. Transfer the pizza to a cutting board, garnish with the Parmigiano, and cut into slices. Serve immediately.

PUTTANESCA PIZZA

WITH STRACCIATELLA

MAKES 1 (12-INCH/30.5-CM) PIZZA

Puttanesca is tomato sauce with salty and briny ingredients added for punch: olives, capers, and anchovies. Great on pasta, it works even better on pizza. When the pizza emerges from the oven, we add stracciatella and eat it immediately.

1	(8-ounce/225-g) ball Pizza Dough (page 31), at room temperature
	Flour, for rolling
3	tablespoons Marinara (page 45)
2	teaspoons chopped Kalamata olives
2	teaspoons capers, drained, rinsed, and chopped
½	teaspoon red wine vinegar, or more as needed
1	anchovy in oil, drained and minced
1	ounce (30 g) stracciatella or burrata cheese
10	basil leaves

At least 30 minutes before baking, place a pizza stone or baking sheet on a baking rack in the top third of the oven, and preheat the oven to 500°F (260°C).

After you have made your dough according to the instructions on pages 31–35, allow the dough to come to room temperature for about 1 hour before making your pizza. Dip the dough into a little flour, shaking off the excess, and set on a clean, lightly floured counter. Start stretching the dough with your hands, turning the ball as you press down the center. Then, using either your hands or a rolling pin (if you're finding stretching the dough by hand to be tricky), work the dough until you form a 12-inch (30.5-cm) circle. If any holes form in the dough, patch them up so the topping does not seep through.

Dust a wooden pizza peel with flour (if you don't have a peel, use an upside-down baking sheet generously dusted with flour) and slide it in under the dough.

In a small bowl, stir together the marinara, olives, capers, vinegar, and anchovy. Using the back of a large spoon, and starting from the center and spiraling your way out, distribute the puttanesca sauce.

Slide the prepared pizza onto the hot pizza stone or baking sheet and bake until the crust is properly browned, about 10 minutes. Check the bottom of the pizza to make sure it has been cooked well—it should be rich brown and burnished. Transfer the pizza to a cutting board, garnish with the stracciatella and basil, and cut into slices. Serve immediately.

PIMENTO CHEESE AND OKRA PIZZA

MAKES 1 (12-INCH/30.5-CM) PIZZA

We wanted to make a straightforward pizza that celebrated the iconic Southern ingredients: pimento cheese and okra. If you're skeptical about how this pie will turn out, still give it a try; I'm confident you will love it. And leftover pimento cheese makes for a great accompaniment to crackers and general *aperitivo* hour snacks.

4	ounces (115 g) okra
	Kosher salt
1	to 2 tablespoons extra virgin-olive oil
1	(8-ounce/225-g) ball Pizza Dough (page 31), at room temperature
	Flour, for rolling
¼	cup (60 g) Pimento Cheese (recipe follows) or store-bought
	Finely grated lemon zest, for garnishing

Preheat the oven to 400°F (205°C). Rinse the okra and dry thoroughly. Trim away the stem ends and the tips, slice in half lengthwise, and place the okra in a large bowl. Salt to taste, and toss with the oil until coated.

Lift the okra from the bowl, draining any excess oil. Arrange on a sheet pan in one layer and roast in the oven for 15 minutes, shaking the pan every 5 minutes, until lightly browned and tender (large okra might take a little longer). Remove from the oven and let cool.

At least 30 minutes before baking the pizza, place a pizza stone or baking sheet on a baking rack in the top third of the oven, and raise the oven temperature to 500°F (260°C).

After you have made your dough according to the instructions on pages 31–35, allow the dough to come to room temperature for about 1 hour before making your pizza. Dip the dough into a little flour, shaking off the excess, and set on a clean, lightly floured counter. Start stretching the dough with your hands, turning the ball as you press down the center. Then, using either your hands or a rolling pin (if you're finding stretching the dough by hand to be tricky), work the dough until you form a 12-inch (30.5-cm) circle. If any holes form in the dough, patch them up so the topping does not seep through.

Dust a wooden pizza peel with flour (if you don't have a peel, use an upside-down baking sheet generously dusted with flour) and slide it in under the dough. Evenly spread the pimento cheese over the crust, and top with roasted okra and a pinch of salt.

Slide the prepared pizza onto the hot pizza stone or baking sheet and bake until the crust is properly browned, about 10 minutes. Check the bottom of the pizza to make sure it has been cooked well—it should be rich brown and burnished. Transfer the pizza to a cutting board, garnish with the lemon zest, and cut into slices. Serve immediately.

PIMENTO CHEESE

MAKES ABOUT ¾ CUP (190 G)

1	cup (110 g) coarsely grated Fontina cheese
¼	cup (60 ml) My Favorite Mayonnaise (page 53) or store-bought
½	roasted red pepper, or store-bought, chopped
1½	teaspoons Calabrian Chile Sauce (page 57)
1½	teaspoons red wine vinegar
¼	teaspoon kosher salt
¼	teaspoon ground black pepper
⅛	teaspoon cayenne pepper
	Very small pinch dried oregano

In a medium bowl, stir together the cheese, mayonnaise, roasted red peppers, chile sauce, vinegar, salt, black pepper, cayenne pepper, and oregano until combined. Use immediately or transfer to a lidded jar and refrigerate for up to 5 days.

SLOW-ROASTED PORK PIZZA

WITH FIG AND GRILLED RED ONION

MAKES 1 (12-INCH/30.5-CM) PIZZA

One of our most popular pizzas, this pie pays homage to the slow-roasted pork popular in many of Miami's Cuban restaurants. Soft, rich meat pairs beautifully with sweet and chewy dried figs, though if you can get your hands on fresh ripe black figs, those would be great as well. A good melting cheese like Fontina complements both the meat and the fruit, and a scattering of arugula leaves lends a peppery bite to these rich flavors.

1   (8-ounce/225-g) ball Pizza Dough (page 31), at room temperature

Flour, for rolling

1   cup (110 g) coarsely grated Fontina cheese

2   tablespoons Grilled Red Onion (page 56)

3   dried black Mission figs, sliced

¼   cup (40 g) coarsely grated Slow-Roasted Pork (page 193)

Kosher salt

½   cup (10 g) arugula

At least 30 minutes before baking, place a pizza stone or baking sheet on a baking rack in the top third of the oven, and preheat the oven to 500°F (260°C).

After you have made your dough according to the instructions on pages 31–35, allow the dough to come to room temperature for about 1 hour before making your pizza. Dip the dough into a little flour, shaking off the excess, and set on a clean, lightly floured counter. Start stretching the dough with your hands, turning the ball as you press down the center. Then, using either your hands or a rolling pin (if you're finding stretching the dough by hand to be tricky), work the dough until you form a 12-inch (30.5-cm) circle. If any holes form in the dough, patch them up so the topping does not seep through.

Dust a wooden pizza peel with flour (if you don't have a peel, use an upside-down baking sheet generously dusted with flour) and slide it in under the dough. Scatter the cheese, onion, figs, and pork on top. Sprinkle with a pinch of salt.

Slide the prepared pizza onto the hot pizza stone or baking sheet and bake until the crust is properly browned, about 10 minutes. Check the bottom of the pizza to make sure it has been cooked well—it should be rich brown and burnished. Transfer the pizza to a cutting board, garnish with the arugula, and cut into slices. Serve immediately.

BLT PIZZA

MAKES 1 (12-INCH/30.5-CM) PIZZA

This is our play on a traditional BLT. We love it as a sandwich, and we figured it would be great as a pizza. Sweet and smoky bacon paired with rich and funky Taleggio make a perfect and potent pair. Peppery arugula, added at the last minute, offers balance and lends an herbaceous green taste.

	Extra-virgin olive oil
2	tablespoons (½-inch/12-mm) pieces bacon
1	(8-ounce/225-g) ball Pizza Dough (page 31), at room temperature
	Flour, for rolling
¼	cup (60 ml) Tomato Sauce (page 44)
1	ounce (30 g) Taleggio cheese, torn into pieces
	Handful arugula leaves, for garnishing

At least 30 minutes before baking, place a pizza stone or baking sheet on a baking rack in the top third of the oven, and preheat the oven to 500°F (260°C).

Meanwhile, heat a pan over medium heat and add a slick of oil. Add the bacon to the pan and gently stir. Cook the bacon, stirring every few minutes, until halfway rendered and the bacon is partially cooked, about 10 minutes. Using a slotted spoon, remove the bacon from the pan to a paper towel–lined plate and set aside.

After you have made your dough according to the instructions on pages 31–35, allow the dough to come to room temperature for about 1 hour before making your pizza. Dip the dough into a little flour, shaking off the excess, and set on a clean, lightly floured counter. Start stretching the dough with your hands, turning the ball as you press down the center. Then, using either your hands or a rolling pin (if you're finding stretching the dough by hand to be tricky), work the dough until you form a 12-inch (30.5-cm) circle. If any holes form in the dough, patch them up so the topping does not seep through.

Dust a wooden pizza peel with flour (if you don't have a peel, use an upside-down baking sheet generously dusted with flour) and slide it in under the dough. Place the tomato sauce, cheese, and bacon—in that order—on top of the dough.

Slide the prepared pizza onto the hot pizza stone or baking sheet and bake until the crust is properly browned, about 10 minutes. Check the bottom of the pizza to make sure it has been cooked well—it should be rich brown and burnished. Transfer the pizza to a cutting board, garnish with the arugula, and cut into slices. Serve immediately.

STRACCIATELLA PIZZA

WITH SPICY ROASTED TOMATO SAUCE AND SCALLION   MAKES 1 (12-INCH/30.5-CM) PIZZA

This is one of my favorite pizzas. While caramelized onions are creamy and rich, the scallions are bold and aggressive, and these two ingredients balance each other out. Garnished with *stracciatella*, this pizza is a celebration of contrasting flavors, textures, and temperatures as the cool, creamy cheese surprises the palate against the hot, fresh-out-of-the-oven pizza.

1   (8-ounce/225-g) ball Pizza Dough (page 31), at room temperature

Flour, for rolling

3   tablespoons Marinara (page 45), or store bought

1   tablespoon Calabrian Chile Sauce (page 57)

2   tablespoons Caramelized Onions (page 58)

2   tablespoons stracciatella cheese

2   tablespoons thinly sliced on the bias scallions

Crushed red pepper

Flaky sea salt

At least 30 minutes before baking, place a pizza stone or baking sheet on a baking rack in the top third of the oven, and preheat the oven to 500°F (260°C).

After you have made your dough according to the instructions on pages 31–35, allow the dough to come to room temperature for about 1 hour before making your pizza. Dip the dough into a little flour, shaking off the excess, and set on a clean, lightly floured counter. Start stretching the dough with your hands, turning the ball as you press down the center. Then, using either your hands or a rolling pin (if you're finding stretching the dough by hand to be tricky), work the dough until you form a 12-inch (30.5-cm) circle. If any holes form in the dough, patch them up so the topping does not seep through.

Dust a wooden pizza peel with flour (if you don't have a peel, use an upside-down baking sheet generously dusted with flour) and slide it in under the dough.

In a small bowl, stir together the marinara and chile sauces until combined. Using the back of a large spoon, and starting from the center and spiraling your way out, distribute the sauce in a thin, even layer. You want to see some of the dough peeking through. Top with the onions.

Slide the prepared pizza onto the hot pizza stone or baking sheet and bake until the crust is properly browned, about 10 minutes. Check the bottom of the pizza to make sure it has been cooked well—it should be rich brown and burnished. Transfer the pizza to a cutting board, garnish with the stracciatella, scallions, crushed red pepper, and salt, and cut into slices. Serve immediately.

BROCCOLINI PIZZA

WITH CALABRIAN CHILE SAUCE

MAKES 1 (12-INCH/30.5-CM) PIZZA

I love broccolini, especially a little charred on the edges after roasting. This is a vegetable-forward pizza that's substantial.

	Kosher salt
1	small bunch broccolini
	Ice, for ice bath
1	(8-ounce/225-g) ball Pizza Dough (page 31), at room temperature
	Flour, for rolling
2	tablespoons Calabrian Chile Sauce (page 57)
½	cup (55 g) coarsely grated Fontina cheese
2	tablespoons cut-on-the-bias scallions
2	tablespoons finely grated Parmigiano-Reggiano cheese

At least 30 minutes before baking, place a pizza stone or baking sheet on a baking rack in the top third of the oven, and preheat the oven to 500°F (260°C).

Meanwhile, prepare an ice bath and bring a medium pot of salted water to a boil. Add the broccolini and blanch until slightly tender, about 3 minutes. Drain and cool in an ice bath. Drain the broccolini and pat dry with clean kitchen towels. Measure out a few stalks of the broccolini and coarsely chop—you will need about ⅓ cup (30 g). Save the rest for other uses—or eat it.

After you have made your dough according to the instructions on pages 31–35, allow the dough to come to room temperature for about 1 hour before making your pizza. Dip the dough into a little flour, shaking off the excess, and set on a clean, lightly floured counter. Start stretching the dough with your hands, turning the ball as you press down the center. Then, using either your hands or a rolling pin (if you're finding stretching the dough by hand to be tricky), work the dough until you form a 12-inch (30.5-cm) circle. If any holes form in the dough, patch them up so the topping does not seep through.

Dust a wooden pizza peel with flour (if you don't have a peel, use an upside-down baking sheet generously dusted with flour) and slide it in under the dough. Using the back of a large spoon, and starting from the center and spiraling your way out, distribute the chile sauce in a thin, even layer. Sprinkle the broccolini and cheese over the dough.

Slide the prepared pizza onto the hot pizza stone or baking sheet and bake until the crust is properly browned, about 10 minutes. Check the bottom of the pizza to make sure it has been cooked well—it should be rich brown and burnished. Transfer the pizza to a cutting board, garnish with the scallions and Parmigiano, and cut into slices. Serve immediately.

FENNEL PIZZA

WITH CARAMELIZED ONION AND
GREEN OLIVES   MAKES 1 (12-INCH/30.5-CM) PIZZA

This fennel pizza was on the menu when we opened Harry's Pizzeria, our first pizza restaurant, and for a long time, it remained as one of our eleven core pies. While it was never a bestseller, this pizza had a loyal following—and the people who loved it, *really* loved it. At the restaurant we use fennel pollen to finish the pizza, but it can be a little tricky to find—and pricey to boot. For your home kitchen, a pinch of freshly ground fennel seeds will do the trick. Trugole is not a widely available cheese, but Auribella, Asiago Fresco, or pecorino fresco make fine substitutes.

1	(8-ounce/225-g) ball Pizza Dough (page 31), at room temperature
	Flour, for rolling
½	cup (55 g) coarsely grated Trugole cheese
¼	cup (55 g) sliced Braised Fennel (page 60)
2	tablespoons chopped pitted Castelvetrano or Cerignola olives
2	tablespoons Caramelized Onions (page 58)
10	basil leaves
	Pinch fennel pollen or freshly ground fennel seeds

At least 30 minutes before baking, place a pizza stone or baking sheet on a baking rack in the top third of the oven, and preheat the oven to 500°F (260°C).

After you have made your dough according to the instructions on pages 31–35, allow the dough to come to room temperature for about 1 hour before making your pizza. Dip the dough into a little flour, shaking off the excess, and set on a clean, lightly floured counter. Start stretching the dough with your hands, turning the ball as you press down the center. Then, using either your hands or a rolling pin (if you're finding stretching the dough by hand to be tricky), work the dough until you form a 12-inch (30.5-cm) circle. If any holes form in the dough, patch them up so the topping does not seep through.

Dust a wooden pizza peel with flour (if you don't have a peel, use an upside-down baking sheet generously dusted with flour) and slide it in under the dough. Scatter the cheese, fennel, olives, and onions on top.

Slide the prepared pizza onto the hot pizza stone or baking sheet and bake until the crust is properly browned, about 10 minutes. Check the bottom of the pizza to make sure it has been cooked well—it should be rich brown and burnished. Transfer the pizza to a cutting board, garnish with the basil and fennel pollen or fennel seeds, and cut into slices. Serve immediately.

PEACH AND GORGONZOLA PIZZA

MAKES 1 (12-INCH/30.5-CM) PIZZA

This is the kind of salad I like to eat—but on a pizza—sweet peaches, salty Gorgonzola, peppery arugula, and earthy-sweet grilled red onion. When looking for peaches for this pie, seek out slightly firm, not-quite-ripe fruit that will hold its shape during baking. Save your super-ripe, juicy peaches for eating raw—you will enjoy them more that way. If you don't have grilled onions on hand, but have caramelized ones, use those instead.

1   (8-ounce/225-g) ball Pizza Dough (page 31), at room temperature

    Flour, for rolling

¼   cup (25 g) coarsely grated Fontina cheese

1   not-quite-ripe peach, halved, pitted, and thinly sliced

2   tablespoons crumbled Gorgonzola cheese

2   tablespoons Grilled Red Onion (page 56) or Caramelized Onions (page 58)

    Handful arugula, for garnishing

At least 30 minutes before baking, place a pizza stone or baking sheet on a baking rack in the top third of the oven, and preheat the oven to 500°F (260°C).

After you have made your dough according to the instructions on pages 31–35, allow the dough to come to room temperature for about 1 hour before making your pizza. Dip the dough into a little flour, shaking off the excess, and set on a clean, lightly floured counter. Start stretching the dough with your hands, turning the ball as you press down the center. Then, using either your hands or a rolling pin (if you're finding stretching the dough by hand to be tricky), work the dough until you form a 12-inch (30.5-cm) circle. If any holes form in the dough, patch them up so the topping does not seep through.

Dust a wooden pizza peel with flour (if you don't have a peel, use an upside-down baking sheet generously dusted with flour) and slide it in under the dough. Scatter the Fontina over the dough and follow with the peach. Sprinkle the Gorgonzola over the peach slices and top with the onion.

Slide the prepared pizza onto the hot pizza stone or baking sheet and bake until the crust is properly browned, about 10 minutes. Check the bottom of the pizza to make sure it has been cooked well—it should be rich brown and burnished. Transfer the pizza to a cutting board, garnish with the arugula, and cut into slices. Serve immediately.

FIG PIZZA

WITH FONTINA, TALEGGIO, AND CRUSHED RED PEPPER MAKES 1 (12-INCH/30.5-CM) PIZZA

I love the combination of contrasting flavors in this sweet and salty pizza: Chewy, sweet figs marry well with ripe Taleggio cheese, and are finished with crushed red pepper and arugula. Such a simple combination, and yet such delicious, complex results. This pizza is also great at room temperature, though good luck with not eating the whole thing immediately.

1	(8-ounce/225-g) ball Pizza Dough (page 31), at room temperature
	Flour, for rolling
3	dried black Mission figs, sliced
½	cup (55 g) coarsely grated Fontina cheese
1	ounce (30 g) Taleggio cheese, cut into small pieces
	Pinch crushed red pepper
	Pinch kosher salt
	Handful arugula, for garnishing

At least 30 minutes before baking, place a pizza stone or baking sheet on a baking rack in the top third of the oven, and preheat the oven to 500°F (260°C).

After you have made your dough according to the instructions on pages 31–35, allow the dough to come to room temperature for about 1 hour before making your pizza. Dip the dough into a little flour, shaking off the excess, and set on a clean, lightly floured counter. Start stretching the dough with your hands, turning the ball as you press down the center. Then, using either your hands or a rolling pin (if you're finding stretching the dough by hand to be tricky), work the dough until you form a 12-inch (30.5-cm) circle. If any holes form in the dough, patch them up so the topping does not seep through.

Dust a wooden pizza peel with flour (if you don't have a peel, use an upside-down baking sheet generously dusted with flour) and slide it in under the dough. Add the figs, Fontina, Taleggio, crushed red pepper, and salt.

Slide the prepared pizza onto the hot pizza stone or baking sheet and bake until the crust is properly browned, about 10 minutes. Check the bottom of the pizza to make sure it has been cooked well—it should be rich brown and burnished. Transfer the pizza to a cutting board, garnish with the arugula, and cut into slices. Serve immediately.

CLAM PIZZA

WITH PRESERVED LEMON, PARMIGIANO-REGGIANO, AND MINT

MAKES 1 (12-INCH/30.5-CM) PIZZA

Everyone needs an excellent clam pizza in his or her toolbox, and this is mine. My favorite touch here is the preserved lemon, which makes for an excellent complement to the briny clams.

1	(8-ounce/225-g) ball Pizza Dough (page 31), at room temperature
	Flour, for rolling
½	cup (110 g) shucked raw clams with brine
¼	cup (25 g) finely grated Parmigiano-Reggiano cheese
¼	cup (25 g) finely grated Pecorino-Romano cheese
1	tablespoon chopped Preserved Lemons rind (page 63) or store-bought
1	tablespoon chopped flat-leaf parsley
	Pinch crushed red pepper
	Extra-virgin olive oil
6	mint leaves, torn

At least 30 minutes before baking, place a pizza stone or baking sheet on a baking rack in the top third of the oven, and preheat the oven to 500°F (260°C).

After you have made your dough according to the instructions on pages 31–35, allow the dough to come to room temperature for about 1 hour before making your pizza. Dip the dough into a little flour, shaking off the excess, and set on a clean, lightly floured counter. Start stretching the dough with your hands, turning the ball as you press down the center. Then, using either your hands or a rolling pin (if you're finding stretching the dough by hand to be tricky), work the dough until you form a 12-inch (30.5-cm) circle. If any holes form in the dough, patch them up so the topping does not seep through.

Dust a wooden pizza peel with flour (if you don't have a peel, use an upside-down baking sheet generously dusted with flour) and slide it in under the dough.

Combine the clams and brine with 1 tablespoon water in a small bowl. Sprinkle the Parmigiano and Pecorino over the dough. Top with the clams with their brine, lemon rind, parsley, and crushed red pepper. Drizzle with a bit of oil.

Slide the prepared pizza onto the hot pizza stone or baking sheet and bake until the crust is properly browned, 8 to 10 minutes. Check the bottom of the pizza to make sure it has been cooked well—it should be rich brown and burnished. Transfer the pizza to a cutting board, garnish with the mint, and cut into slices. Serve immediately.

PROSCIUTTO COTTO PIZZA

MAKES 1 (12-INCH/30.5-CM) PIZZA

When asparagus appears at greenmarket stands, we know spring has arrived. This pizza is an ode to the season, with bits of ham and fresh asparagus bound together by a sharp, rich pecorino cream. Using a vegetable peeler on thick asparagus stalks yields festive-looking ribbons, lightly sautéed onions balance out the salty ham, resulting in a delicious seasonal pie.

	Extra-virgin olive oil
2	tablespoons chopped yellow onion
1	(8-ounce/225-g) ball Pizza Dough (page 31), at room temperature
	Flour, for rolling
¼	cup (60 ml) Pecorino Crema (page 52)
¼	cup (40 g) diced prosciutto cotto
2	thick asparagus stalks

At least 30 minutes before baking, place a pizza stone or baking sheet on a baking rack in the top third of the oven, and preheat the oven to 500°F (260°C).

Meanwhile, in a small sauté pan, warm a slick of oil over medium heat. Add the onion and cook, stirring, until softened and translucent, 4 to 5 minutes. Do not let the onion put on color. Remove from the heat and set aside.

After you have made your dough according to the instructions on pages 31–35, allow the dough to come to room temperature for about 1 hour before making your pizza. Dip the dough into a little flour, shaking off the excess, and set on a clean, lightly floured counter. Start stretching the dough with your hands, turning the ball as you press down the center. Then, using either your hands or a rolling pin (if you're finding stretching the dough by hand to be tricky), work the dough until you form a 12-inch (30.5-cm) circle. If any holes form in the dough, patch them up so the topping does not seep through.

Dust a wooden pizza peel with flour (if you don't have a peel, use an upside-down baking sheet generously dusted with flour) and slide it in under the dough. Evenly spread the crema over the dough, then top with the prosciutto. Using a vegetable peeler, shave the asparagus into ribbons, then place on top of the prosciutto, followed by the onion.

Slide the prepared pizza onto the hot pizza stone or baking sheet and bake until the crust is properly browned, about 10 minutes. Check the bottom of the pizza to make sure it has been cooked well—it should be rich brown and burnished. Transfer the pizza to a cutting board and cut into slices. Serve immediately.

MERGUEZ PIZZA

MAKES 1 (12-INCH/30.5-CM) PIZZA

I wanted to have a sausage pizza on the menu, and one inspired by Middle Eastern flavors—merguez pizza was born. If you're skeptical about the combination of *merguez* (a spiced Middle Eastern sausage), halloumi, and mint on pizza, you need to trust me, as this unusual pie is an absolute winner, flavorful and delicious. So make some merguez for dinner (see page 199), save a few pieces for this incredible combination of flavors, and give this pizza a try. I'm positive you'll make it again and again.

1   (8-ounce/225-g) ball Pizza Dough (page 31), at room temperature

    Flour, for rolling

¼   cup (60 ml) Tomato Sauce (page 44)

1   teaspoon harissa paste, plus more as needed

1   golf ball–size piece uncooked merguez (see page 199) or store-bought, crumbled

½   cup (55 g) coarsely grated Halloumi cheese

2   tablespoons thinly sliced on bias scallions

1   sprig fresh mint, leaves picked

At least 30 minutes before baking, place a pizza stone or baking sheet on a baking rack in the top third of the oven, and preheat the oven to 500°F (260°C).

After you have made your dough according to the instructions on pages 31–35, allow the dough to come to room temperature for about 1 hour before making your pizza. Dip the dough into a little flour, shaking off the excess, and set on a clean, lightly floured counter. Start stretching the dough with your hands, turning the ball as you press down the center. Then, using either your hands or a rolling pin (if you're finding stretching the dough by hand to be tricky), work the dough until you form a 12-inch (30.5-cm) circle. If any holes form in the dough, patch them up so the topping does not seep through.

Dust a wooden pizza peel with flour (if you don't have a peel, use an upside-down baking sheet generously dusted with flour) and slide it in under the dough. In a small bowl, stir together the tomato sauce and harissa until combined. Using the back of a large spoon, and starting from the center and spiraling your way out, distribute the mixture, in a thin, even layer. Follow with the merguez and cheese.

Slide the prepared pizza onto the hot pizza stone or baking sheet and bake until the crust is properly browned, about 10 minutes. Check the bottom of the pizza to make sure it has been cooked well—it should be rich brown and burnished. Transfer the pizza to a cutting board, garnish with the scallions and mint, and cut into slices. Serve immediately.

BACON, EGG, AND CHEESE PIZZA

MAKES 1 (12-INCH/30.5-CM) PIZZA

One of the cornerstones of American food is the beloved bacon, egg, and cheese sandwich. And, as I always say, what's good on a sandwich has to be good on pizza.

Extra-virgin olive oil

2 ounces (55 g) bacon, cut into ½-inch (12-mm) pieces

1 (8-ounce/225-g) ball Pizza Dough (page 31), at room temperature

Flour, for rolling

½ cup (55 g) coarsely grated Fontina cheese

1 large egg

2 tablespoons chopped scallions

Pinch crushed red pepper, for garnishing (optional)

Flaky sea salt, for garnishing (optional)

Hot sauce or sriracha, for serving (optional)

At least 30 minutes before baking, place a pizza stone or baking sheet on a baking rack in the top third of the oven, and preheat the oven to 500°F (260°C).

Meanwhile, cook the bacon (see page 108).

After you have made your dough according to the instructions on pages 31–35, allow the dough to come to room temperature for about 1 hour before making your pizza. Dip the dough into a little flour, shaking off the excess, and set on a clean, lightly floured counter. Start stretching the dough with your hands, turning the ball as you press down the center. Then, using either your hands or a rolling pin (if you're finding stretching the dough by hand to be tricky), work the dough until you form a 12-inch (30.5-cm) circle. If any holes form in the dough, patch them up so the topping does not seep through.

Dust a wooden pizza peel with flour (if you don't have a peel, use an upside-down baking sheet generously dusted with flour) and slide it in under the dough. Top with the cheese and scatter the bacon on top.

Slide the prepared pizza onto the hot pizza stone or baking sheet. Using the back of a large spoon, make a divot in the center of pizza, and crack the egg into it. Bake until the egg white is set but the yolk is still liquid, and the crust is properly browned, about 8 minutes. (Depending on how hot your oven runs, you may need to adjust the cooking time, so watch your egg carefully.) Check the bottom of the pizza to make sure it has been cooked well—it should be rich brown and burnished. Transfer the pizza to a cutting board and garnish with the scallions, crushed red pepper (if using), and salt (if using). Cut into slices and serve immediately with hot sauce, if desired.

SOPPRESSATA PIZZA

WITH MOZZARELLA, CALABRIAN CHILE SAUCE, AND SCALLION

MAKES 1 (12-INCH/30.5-CM) PIZZA

According to multiple sources, the most popular pizza topping in the United States is pepperoni. While we don't serve pepperoni pizza, we do offer something even better. We swap out pepperoni for the more complex, spicy soppressata. And if you're into a spicy-sweet melding of flavors, I recommend a drizzle of honey at the end!

1	(8-ounce/225-g) ball Pizza Dough (page 31), at room temperature
	Flour, for rolling
3	tablespoons Tomato Sauce (page 44)
2	tablespoons Calabrian Chile Sauce (page 57)
¼	cup (25 g) coarsely grated Fontina cheese
¼	cup (30 g) torn fresh mozzarella cheese
10	small, thin slices spicy soppressata
2	tablespoons chopped scallions
	Honey, for garnishing (optional)

At least 30 minutes before baking, place a pizza stone or baking sheet on a baking rack in the top third of the oven, and preheat the oven to 500°F (260°C).

After you have made your dough according to the instructions on pages 31–35, allow the dough to come to room temperature for about 1 hour before making your pizza. Dip the dough into a little flour, shaking off the excess, and set on a clean, lightly floured counter. Start stretching the dough with your hands, turning the ball as you press down the center. Then, using either your hands or a rolling pin (if you're finding stretching the dough by hand to be tricky), work the dough until you form a 12-inch (30.5-cm) circle. If any holes form in the dough, patch them up so the topping does not seep through.

Dust a wooden pizza peel with flour (if you don't have a peel, use an upside-down baking sheet generously dusted with flour) and slide it in under the dough.

In a small bowl, stir together the tomato and chile sauces until combined. Using the back of a large spoon, and starting from the center and spiraling your way out, distribute the sauce in a thin, even layer. You want to see some of the dough peeking through. Scatter the Fontina and mozzarella on top and then soppressata.

Slide the prepared pizza onto the hot pizza stone or baking sheet and bake until the crust is properly browned, about 10 minutes. Check the bottom of the pizza to make sure it has been cooked well—it should be rich brown and burnished. Transfer the pizza to a cutting board, garnish with the scallions, and drizzle with honey, if using. Cut into slices and serve immediately.

ZUCCHINI PIZZA

MAKES 1 (12-INCH/30.5-CM) PIZZA

This pizza tastes so bright and fresh, you won't be able to stop eating it. When they're in season, swap out the zucchini for half a dozen fresh zucchini blossoms for a beautiful and delicious twist.

2	tablespoons Homemade Ricotta (page 150) or store-bought
2	tablespoons extra-virgin olive oil
2	oil-packed anchovies, pounded into paste
1	(8-ounce/225-g) ball Pizza Dough (page 31), at room temperature
	Flour, for rolling
½	medium zucchini, shaved into wide ribbons with a mandoline or vegetable peeler
½	Roasted Lemon (page 90) or fresh lemon, finely chopped
¼	cup (25 g) finely grated Grana Padano cheese
¼	teaspoon crushed red pepper
6	basil leaves, torn
1	tablespoon chopped fresh mint

At least 30 minutes before baking, place a pizza stone or baking sheet on a baking rack in the top third of the oven, and preheat the oven to 500°F (260°C).

After you have made your dough according to the instructions on pages 31–35, allow the dough to come to room temperature for about 1 hour before making your pizza. Dip the dough into a little flour, shaking off the excess, and set on a clean, lightly floured counter. Start stretching the dough with your hands, turning the ball as you press down the center. Then, using either your hands or a rolling pin (if you're finding stretching the dough by hand to be tricky), work the dough until you form a 12-inch (30.5-cm) circle. If any holes form in the dough, patch them up so the topping does not seep through.

Dust a wooden pizza peel with flour (if you don't have a peel, use an upside-down baking sheet generously dusted with flour) and slide it in under the dough.

In a small bowl, stir together the ricotta, oil, and anchovies until combined. Spread the ricotta mixture across the pizza, then add 4 or 5 ribbons of zucchini, twisting them once or twice like ribbons. Follow with the lemon, sprinkle the Grana Padano on top, and scatter the crushed red pepper, basil, and mint over the cheese. Slide the prepared pizza onto the hot pizza stone or baking sheet and bake until the crust is properly browned, about 10 minutes. Check the bottom of the pizza to make sure it has been cooked well—it should be rich brown and burnished. Transfer the pizza to a cutting board, cut into slices, and serve immediately.

PASTRAMI ON RYE PIZZA

MAKES 1 (12-INCH/30.5-CM) PIZZA

In 2017, we did a pop-up with New York's famed Katz's Delicatessen and made pastrami pizza. We started with a rye crust (see page 37) and made a base of mustard and mayonnaise, which we topped with pastrami and sauerkraut. The pizza was a hit, and we went through about a thousand pounds of pastrami in a single night. We plan to do another pop-up with Katz's soon to re-create the magic.

1	(8-ounce/225-g) ball Rye Pizza Dough (page 37), at room temperature
	Flour, for rolling
2	teaspoons spicy brown mustard
2	tablespoons My Favorite Mayonnaise (page 53) or store-bought
1	tablespoon well-shaken buttermilk
	Kosher salt
	Freshly ground black pepper
½	cup (55 g) coarsely grated Gruyère cheese
¼	cup (40 g) sauerkraut
3	thin slices pastrami
1	scallion, cut on the bias

At least 30 minutes before baking, place a pizza stone or baking sheet on a baking rack in the top third of the oven, and preheat the oven to 500°F (260°C).

After you have made your dough according to the instructions on pages 37–38, allow the dough to come to room temperature for about 1 hour before making your pizza. Dip the dough into a little flour, shaking off the excess, and set on a clean, lightly floured counter. Start stretching the dough with your hands, turning the ball as you press down the center. Then, using either your hands or a rolling pin (if you're finding stretching the dough by hand to be tricky), work the dough until you form a 12-inch (30.5-cm) circle. If any holes form in the dough, patch them up so the topping does not seep through.

Dust a wooden pizza peel with flour (if you don't have a peel, use an upside-down baking sheet generously dusted with flour) and slide it in under the dough.

In a small bowl, whisk together the mustard, mayonnaise, and buttermilk until incorporated. Season to taste with salt and pepper. Spread the mustard sauce on the dough, then evenly scatter the cheese, sauerkraut, and pastrami on top.

Slide the prepared pizza onto the hot pizza stone or baking sheet and bake until the crust is properly browned, about 10 minutes. Check the bottom of the pizza to make sure it has been cooked well—it should be rich brown and burnished. Transfer the pizza to a cutting board, garnish with scallions, and cut into slices. Serve immediately.

BITTER GREENS PIZZA

MAKES 1 (12-INCH/30.5-CM) PIZZA

This pizza is as beautiful as it is tasty—especially right before you bake it, as shown opposite. The bright greens wilt in the oven and come out like pressed flowers in a book—stunning.

1	(8-ounce/225-g) ball Pizza Dough (page 31), at room temperature
	Flour, for rolling
2	tablespoons Peperonata (see page 186)
1	to 2 teaspoons Calabrian Chile Sauce (page 57)
1	to 2 teaspoons red wine vinegar, or to taste
1	teaspoon honey
¼	cup (60 ml) Béchamel (page 48)
¼	cup (25 g) finely grated Parmigiano-Reggiano cheese
2	large handfuls baby mustard, dandelion, or other sturdy bitter greens
	Pinch kosher salt

At least 30 minutes before baking, place a pizza stone or baking sheet on a baking rack in the top third of the oven, and preheat the oven to 500°F (260°C).

After you have made your dough according to the instructions on pages 31–35, allow the dough to come to room temperature for about 1 hour before making your pizza. Dip the dough into a little flour, shaking off the excess, and set on a clean, lightly floured counter. Start stretching the dough with your hands, turning the ball as you press down the center. Then, using either your hands or a rolling pin (if you're finding stretching the dough by hand to be tricky), work the dough until you form a 12-inch (30.5-cm) circle. If any holes form in the dough, patch them up so the topping does not seep through.

Dust a wooden pizza peel with flour (if you don't have a peel, use an upside-down baking sheet generously dusted with flour) and slide it in under the dough.

In a small bowl, stir together the peperonata, chile sauce, vinegar, and honey until combined and set aside.

Evenly spread the béchamel over the dough. Add the cheese, dab on the peperonata mixture, and top with the greens. Sprinkle the salt all over.

Slide the prepared pizza onto the hot pizza stone or baking sheet and bake until the crust is properly browned, about 10 minutes. Check the bottom of the pizza to make sure it has been cooked well—it should be rich brown and burnished. Transfer the pizza to a cutting board, cut into slices, and serve immediately.

ONE CANNOT LIVE ON PIZZA ALONE

THINGS TO EAT WITH YOUR PIZZA

PART III

███

MEATBALLS

MAKES ABOUT 20 MEATBALLS; SERVES 4 TO 6

These are pretty classic Italian meatballs—a mixture of beef for flavor and pork for fat and tenderness. So, while I don't have a revolutionary new meatball recipe for you, I do have a few important tips to keep in mind as you make your balls. First, bread soaked in milk keeps the meatballs light and fluffy. Second, when shaping the balls, don't overpack them, as they become dense when compressed too much. Third, if your meatballs are not perfect little spheres, that's OK—they're supposed to look rustic. However, if you want them to look super even, the chilling of the meat mixture before shaping the meatballs helps a lot to achieve that perfect shape. Serve them on their own as a starter, with polenta (see page 193), or on top of spaghetti (what's more American than that)? And leftover meatballs, if you have them (lucky you), are great on pizza (see page 85), or in part of a classic sub with provolone and peppers and onions.

- ¾ cup (180 ml) whole milk
- 2 (½-inch-wide/12-mm-wide) slices white Pullman loaf or challah bread, crusts removed
- ⅓ cup (30 g) finely grated Parmigiano-Reggiano cheese
- ¼ cup (13 g) finely chopped flat-leaf parsley
- 2 large garlic cloves, minced
- 2 large eggs
- 1 large egg yolk
- 1 tablespoon kosher salt
- 1 teaspoon freshly ground black pepper
- 1 pound (455 g) ground beef
- 8 ounces (225 g) ground veal
- 8 ounces (225 g) ground pork
- Olive oil, for frying
- Marinara (page 45), for cooking
- Finely grated Parmigiano-Reggiano, for serving

In a large bowl, pour the milk over the bread and soak, until completely saturated, about 10 minutes.

Add the cheese, parsley, garlic, eggs, salt, and pepper, and mix thoroughly with your hands until the mixture is uniform.

Add the beef, veal, and pork and, using your hands, mix thoroughly to combine. Cover the bowl with plastic wrap and refrigerate until the meat is completely chilled, at least 2 hours and up to 24 hours. You will have an easier time shaping the meatballs if you're working with a cold meat mixture.

When ready to cook the meatballs, preheat the oven to 300°F (150°C). Use a ¼ cup (60 ml) scoop to form the meatballs. Place on a parchment-lined sheet pan while you work with the remaining meat mixture.

In a large pan, add enough oil to cover the bottom of the pan and warm over medium-high heat until the oil is shimmering. Add the meatballs without overcrowding (you will need to do this in batches) and pan-fry until browned on all sides, about 15 minutes per batch. (Make sure the meatballs put on deep brown color and aren't just getting light grayish-brown. Properly seared, the meatballs will better maintain their shape in the oven and taste much better.) Transfer the fried meatballs to a paper towel–lined tray. Repeat with the remaining meatballs.

Transfer all the browned meatballs to an ovenproof pot and cover with the marinara. Cover the pot with a piece of parchment paper and place the lid on top. Transfer the pot to the oven and cook the meatballs in the sauce for about 2 hours.

Divide the meatballs and the sauce among four to six bowls and serve with some grated Parmigiano.

OVEN-ROASTED CHICKEN WINGS

WITH AGRODOLCE GLAZE AND
ROSEMARY CREMA SERVES 4 TO 6

This is our Italian-inspired, healthier answer to buffalo wings. Instead of deep-frying, we bake our wings and then glaze them with *agrodolce* sauce. In place of a blue cheese dip, we serve the wings with some rosemary crema, which pairs perfectly with the sweet-and-sour flavors. If you find yourself with leftover glaze, use it as marinade for meat and fish, or toss vegetables in it before roasting—delicious!

	Olive oil
2	pounds (910 g) chicken wings
2	teaspoons kosher salt
½	cup (120 ml) Agrodolce Glaze (recipe follows)
½	cup (120 ml) Rosemary Crema (page 51), for dipping

Preheat the oven to 425°F (220°C). Line a shallow baking pan with foil and lightly brush it with oil.

In a large bowl, toss the wings with the salt, then spread them evenly on the baking pan. Roast for about 35 minutes, turning once, until cooked through. Remove from the oven and let cool slightly.

Preheat the broiler on high.

Toss the wings with ¼ cup (60 ml) of the agrodolce glaze and broil for about 2 minutes, or until the glaze is thickened and glistens on the wings. Transfer to a bowl, toss with the remaining ¼ cup (60 ml) glaze, and serve with the rosemary crema on the side.

AGRODOLCE GLAZE

MAKES ABOUT 1⅓ CUPS (315 ML)

1	cup (240 ml) mild honey
2	tablespoons Calabrian Chile Sauce (page 57)
2	tablespoons red wine vinegar
2	teaspoons canola oil
1	teaspoon kosher salt
½	teaspoon ground fennel seeds

In a container with tall sides (such as a 1-quart/1-L deli container), whisk together the honey, chile sauce, vinegar, oil, salt, and fennel with a fork. Using an immersion blender, blend until thoroughly combined. Cover and refrigerate until needed, for up to 1 week.

POLENTA FRIES

WITH SPICY KETCHUP
MAKES 2 DOZEN FRIES; SERVES 4 TO 6

These fries are addictive and impossible to stop eating, particularly thanks to the spicy ketchup that comes with them. I spent the early part of my career cooking Italian food, and when I began working for Wolfgang Puck, I started to realize that it's OK to break all kinds of perceived cooking rules and make food that just tastes good, whether or not the flavors are expected or not. I'm pretty sure that serving ketchup with polenta in Italy is a punishable offense, never mind serving ketchup with cilantro and jalapeño. Any day now, the Italian food police just might come after me. On paper it doesn't make any sense, but try it for yourself and see. Leftover spicy ketchup is great with fries, hot dogs—what have you.

1	quart (960 ml) whole milk
3	tablespoons (45 g) unsalted butter
2	cups (370 g) yellow medium-grind cornmeal (not quick-cooking)
½	cup (50 g) finely grated Grana Padano or Parmigiano-Reggiano cheese
½	cup (50 g) finely grated Pecorino-Romano cheese
1	teaspoon kosher salt, plus more as needed
½	teaspoon freshly ground black pepper, plus more as needed
	Canola oil, for frying
	Spicy Ketchup (recipe follows)

Line a 9 by 13-inch (23 by 33-cm) baking dish with plastic wrap, letting the excess hang over the sides. Set aside.

In a large pot over medium heat, bring the milk, 1 cup (240 ml) water, and the butter to a simmer. Gradually whisk in the cornmeal in a slow steady stream. Reduce the heat to medium-low. Cook, stirring often with a wooden spoon, until the polenta is *very* thick and pulls away from the sides of the pot, about 15 minutes. (At this point the polenta should be thick enough that it should take some effort to stir. Consider it a workout for your forearms.) Remove from the heat. Stir in the Grano Padano or Parmigiano and the Pecorino until incorporated. Season with the salt and pepper. Taste and adjust the seasonings as needed.

Transfer the polenta to the prepared baking dish, spreading evenly with a silicone spatula to a thickness of about ½ inch (12 mm). Let it cool to room temperature, then cover it with plastic wrap and refrigerate until completely cool and firm, at least 1 hour or, better yet, overnight. It is important for polenta to set up and get dense; this will allow you to cut it into strips that won't fall apart in the hot oil when you fry them.

In a deep pot set over medium-high heat or countertop electric fryer, heat 3 inches (7.5 cm) oil to 350°F (175°C). If you don't have a deep-fry thermometer, stick the end of a wooden spoon or chopstick in the oil—if bubbles start to form around the end, the oil is hot enough.

Grab the plastic wrap overhang and lift the polenta out of the baking dish onto a cutting board. Flip the polenta over to remove and discard the plastic wrap. Cut the polenta into thirds lengthwise, then crosswise into sticks. You should wind up with 24 large, Jenga-like pieces, about ¾ inch (2 cm) wide by 4 inches (10 cm) long.

Working in batches of six, so you are not overcrowding the pot, put the polenta sticks in a fryer basket or a spider strainer and carefully lower into the hot oil. Fry the polenta sticks for 3 to 5 minutes, until golden brown and crispy. Transfer them to a paper towel–lined platter to drain. Season lightly with salt while the fries are still hot—this will allow the salt to adhere to the fries. Stack the polenta fries like Jenga on a serving platter and serve immediately with spicy ketchup.

SPICY KETCHUP

MAKES 2 CUPS (480 ML)

1	tablespoon extra-virgin olive oil
½	small yellow onion, chopped
2	garlic cloves, chopped
½	jalapeño chile, seeded and chopped, plus more as needed
½	teaspoon kosher salt, plus more as needed
¼	teaspoon freshly ground black pepper, plus more as needed
1	cup (240 ml) ketchup
1	tablespoon chopped cilantro leaves

Warm a small skillet over medium heat until hot. Coat with the oil, then add the onion, garlic, jalapeño, salt, and pepper. Cook, stirring, until the onions soften and start to put on a little color, about 3 minutes.

Remove from the heat and scrape the vegetable mixture into a food processor fitted with a blade. Pulse until combined but not completely smooth; you want to retain some chunky texture. Transfer the vegetables to a bowl and add the ketchup and cilantro; stir until thoroughly combined. Taste and adjust the seasonings if necessary. The ketchup will keep, refrigerated, for up to 1 week.

CAPONATA

WITH FOCACCIA   MAKES 2 QUARTS (2 L)

Caponata is misunderstood in the States, as many don't realize that it needs to be both sweet *and* sour (in Italian there's a wonderful word for that—*agrodolce*). Caponata is traditionally served at room temperature with some warm focaccia, and I think it's one of the best ways to kick off a meal. Keep in mind, when making the plump raisins, don't overcook them or the raisins will turn gummy.

For the plump raisins:

- ½ cup (75 g) dark raisins
- ¼ cup (60 ml) extra-virgin olive oil
- ½ sprig rosemary

For the caponata:

- 2 red bell peppers
- 2 red onions, peeled, halved, and sliced into ¼-inch (6-mm) half-moons
- 2 large beefsteak tomatoes (about 18 ounces/510 g)
- 2 large Italian eggplants (about 3½ pounds/1.6 kg), peeled and cut into 1-inch (2.5-cm) dice
- ¼ cup (60 ml) extra-virgin olive oil, plus more for drizzling and greasing
- 1 tablespoon kosher salt, plus more as needed
- ¼ teaspoon freshly ground black pepper, plus more as needed
- 2 garlic cloves, minced
- ⅔ cup (105 g) Castelvetrano olives, pitted and sliced
- ⅔ cup (30 g) basil leaves, roughly chopped
- ⅓ cup (60 g) plump raisins (recipe follows)
- 3 tablespoons champagne vinegar
- Focaccia (recipe follows) or store-bought, warmed
- Chopped flat-leaf parsley, for garnishing

Make the plump raisins:
Preheat the oven to 350°F (175°F).

   In an ovenproof dish, combine the raisins, oil, rosemary, and 2 tablespoons water and cover tightly with aluminum foil. Transfer the dish to the oven and cook for 15 minutes, or until the raisins are plump and soft. Remove from the oven, let cool, and set aside. If not using the raisins immediately, transfer them with their cooking liquid to a container, cover, and refrigerate for up to 5 days.

Make the caponata:

Raise the oven temperature to 500°F (260°C). Place the whole red bell peppers on a sheet pan and place in the oven for 25 to 30 minutes, turning them twice during roasting, until the skins are completely wrinkled and the peppers are charred. Remove the pan from the oven, transfer the bell peppers to a nonreactive bowl, and immediately cover it tightly with plastic wrap. Set aside the bell peppers for 30 minutes, or until they are cool enough to handle. Lower the oven temperature to 425°F (220°C).

Once the bell peppers are cool, peel, stem and quarter them, then discard their peels and seeds. Return the bell peppers to the bowl along with any juices that have collected. (If not using right away, cover with oil and refrigerate for up to 2 weeks.)

Lightly grease four half-sheet baking pans. Spread the onions on one, spread the tomatoes on another, and divide the eggplant between two half-sheet pans. Drizzle the vegetables with the oil (be generous with the eggplant, as it loves oil) and season them with the salt and pepper. Transfer the pans to the oven. Roast for 20 to 25 minutes for the onions and tomatoes, until the onions are wilted and starting to caramelize, and the tomatoes start to split down the side; roast the eggplant for 30 to 35 minutes, until it is nicely browned and very soft. Remove the vegetables from the oven and let them cool until just warm to the touch. Halve and seed the tomatoes, then chop into medium dice. Transfer all the roasted vegetables to a large bowl.

In a small saucepan, warm ¼ cup (60 ml) oil over medium-low heat until shimmering. Add the garlic and cook, swirling the pan, until fragrant and toasted, 1 to 2 minutes. Do not let the garlic burn. Remove from the heat and transfer to the bowl with the roasted vegetables. Add the olives, basil, raisins, and vinegar, and let cool to room temperature.

Serve the caponata with warmed focaccia. Drizzle the focaccia with oil, top with the caponata, and garnish with the parsley.

FOCACCIA

SERVES 12

1	tablespoon extra-virgin olive oil, plus more for greasing the sheet
1	(8-ounce/225-g) ball Pizza Dough (page 31), at room temperature
1	tablespoon chopped rosemary leaves
¾	teaspoon kosher salt
⅛	teaspoon freshly ground black pepper

Preheat the oven to 450°F (230°C).

Grease a baking sheet with oil and place the pizza dough on top. Press the dough down with your fingertips into a loosely shaped oval and drizzle with the 1 tablespoon oil. Top the dough with the rosemary, salt, and pepper. Bake for 12 to 15 minutes, until golden brown. Remove from the oven and let cool on the baking rack until warm to the touch. Serve with caponata.

HOMEMADE RICOTTA

MAKES 1 QUART (1 L)

There are myriad ways to make ricotta, and this is mine. After playing around with lemon juice, vinegar, and cultures to curdle the milk, I found that the buttermilk made the ricotta richer as well as tangier. The secret to making good ricotta couldn't be simpler: Buy good milk and buttermilk; quality ingredients will yield a superior result. Also, be patient: Low and slow is the best way to heat milk and buttermilk—whatever you do, don't rush it. Use it on pizza (see page 93), spread it on toast with honey and cracked black pepper, or use it to top off pasta, and see just how easy it is to make—you may never go back to the store-bought stuff.

2 quarts (2 L) whole milk

2 cups (480 ml) buttermilk

1 teaspoon kosher salt, plus more as needed

In a large pot, combine the milk, buttermilk, and salt and warm over low heat. Don't rush the process—this could take about 1 hour, so be patient. Stir the mixture often to prevent scorching on the bottom. Be sure to monitor the heat, and watch carefully for milk curds to start forming and separating from the whey—this should start happening about 15 minutes after you see the first tiny bubbles appear on the surface. Remove from the heat and let the mixture stand, undisturbed, for about 10 minutes.

Strain the curds through a cheese cloth–lined sieve, reserving 2 cups (480 ml) of the whey. Let the ricotta drain until it is completely cooled off, 2 to 3 hours. Transfer the ricotta to a container large enough to hold it.

If the ricotta feels too stiff (not easily spreadable), add some of the reserved whey, 1 tablespoon at a time, until you get to the right consistency. Season with more salt, if desired, and stir to combine until uniform. Cover the container and refrigerate until cold, or for up to 1 week.

151

MARINATED OLIVES

MAKES ABOUT 1 QUART (1 L)

I like to buy olives at the olive bar in my grocery store and doctor them up—just a few added ingredients make store-bought olives really shine. Because marinated olives are so easy to make, you should always have some on hand. They're perfect should unexpected company show up, or if you just want to have a small snack with your cocktail while making dinner.

1¼	cups (300 ml) extra-virgin olive oil
2	sprigs rosemary
¾	teaspoon fennel seeds
¾	teaspoon crushed red pepper
2	cups (310 g) mixed olives
3	garlic cloves, peeled
1½	teaspoons finely grated orange zest
1½	teaspoons finely grated lemon zest

In a small pot, combine the oil, rosemary, fennel, and crushed red pepper, and warm the ingredients over low heat for about 10 minutes, or until the oil is infused.

While the oil mixture is warming up, rinse the olives under cold running water. Drain the olives thoroughly and transfer to a 1-quart (1-L) container.

Remove the oil from the heat and let cool slightly. Stir in the garlic, orange zest, and lemon zest, and then pour the oil mixture over the olives. Let the olives marinate at room temperature for 2 hours, then cover and refrigerate until needed and for up to 2 weeks.

TOMATO BREAD SOUP

SERVES 4

This simple, unfussy soup is surprisingly filling, thanks to the addition of bread at the end (a perfect use for that day-old bread you've got lying around). Blending the oil into the base builds body, as well as a smooth, luxurious consistency, which imitates the richness of cream. Perfect on its own, or accompanied by grilled cheese sandwiches, this soup is an antidote to a cold, wet day—a soothing, uplifting meal when a little extra comfort is just the necessary thing.

¼	cup plus 2 tablespoons (90 ml) extra-virgin olive oil, plus more for garnishing
1	small onion, coarsely chopped
3	garlic cloves, coarsely chopped
	Kosher salt
	Freshly ground black pepper
6	large beefsteak tomatoes (about 4 pounds/1.8 kg), cores removed and cut into large chunks, juices reserved
2	cups (90 g) hand-torn pieces of day-old bread
3	large basil leaves, plus more for garnishing

Place a soup pot over medium-high heat and add 2 tablespoons of the oil. When the oil is shimmering, add the onion and garlic and sauté for about 3 minutes, until the onion is translucent; season with the salt and pepper. Add the tomatoes and their juices and 2 cups (480 ml) water. Bring the mixture to a boil, then reduce the heat so the soup is at a simmer, cover, and cook until the tomatoes begin to soften and break down into a chunky pulp, about 10 minutes.

Remove the lid, and toss in the bread and basil leaves. Cook, uncovered, stirring gently, until the bread gets very soft and absorbs the liquid, about 5 minutes. Push the bread pieces down with a wooden spoon if they float to the top. Reduce the heat to low if it's not already, cover, and cook until the tomatoes have completely collapsed and the bread has mostly disintegrated, another 15 minutes.

Remove the pot from the heat and stir in ¼ cup (60 ml) oil. Using an immersion blender, purée the soup until smooth. Taste and adjust seasonings, if needed.

To serve, ladle soup into bowls, drizzle with more oil, and garnish with basil.

SHORT RIB AND FARRO SOUP

SERVES 6

This is a play on traditional beef and barley soup. If you have some leftover short ribs (see page 197) around, and you aren't going to put them on pizza (see page 79), using them in this soup will blow you away with its depth of flavor. Deep, roasted notes from the meat give this soup structure, and the farro offers a satisfying bite. Don't skimp on the mirepoix ingredients—your holy trinity of carrots, onions, and celery—that's where the soup gets a great deal of its flavor. And if you don't have short ribs on hand, you use whatever leftover roasted meat you've got, especially if it's bone-in.

Extra-virgin olive oil

4   cups (500 g) diced onions

2   cups (280 g) diced carrots

2   cups (200 g) diced celery

2   tablespoons kosher salt, plus more
    as needed

½   teaspoon freshly ground black pepper, plus
    more as needed

8   ounces (225 g) cooked Short Rib (page 197)

1   cup (200 g) farro

½   bunch thyme sprigs, plus more for
    garnishing

1   bay leaf

In a heavy-bottomed pot, add enough oil to generously coat the bottom. Set the pot over medium heat and warm the oil until it shimmers, then add the onions, carrots, celery, salt, and pepper. Cook, stirring, until the vegetables soften, 7 to 8 minutes. Make sure the vegetables do not put on color.

Add the meat, farro, thyme (reserve 1 sprig for garnish), bay leaf, and 10 cups (2.4 L) water and bring to a boil. Immediately reduce the heat so the soup is at a simmer, and cook, uncovered, for about 30 minutes, until the farro is al dente and the soup has a pronounced flavor of vegetables and beef.

Discard the bay leaf and thyme sprigs (the thyme leaves will have come off into the soup). Ladle the soup into bowls, garnish with thyme, and serve immediately.

WHITE BEAN AND CHORIZO SOUP

SERVES 6

White beans and smoky Spanish chorizo are a perfect pairing, and the resulting soup they create together is comforting and filling. If you prefer to cook your own beans, by all means, soak some beans the night before and cook them separately, adding them as you would the canned. See page 198 for my method of cooking beans. But for extra convenience and a perfect weekday meal, canned beans will come through and save you loads of time.

1	tablespoon extra-virgin olive oil
4	cups (500 g) diced onions
2	cups (280 g) diced carrots
2	cups (200 g) diced celery
2	tablespoons kosher salt
½	teaspoon freshly ground black pepper
2	cans cannellini beans (15.5 ounces/ 439 g each), rinsed and drained
½	bunch thyme sprigs
1	bay leaf
8	cups (480 g) chopped escarole
2	cups (300 g) diced dry Spanish chorizo
	Cilantro leaves, for garnishing
	Slivered scallions, for garnishing

In a large heavy-bottomed pot, combine the oil, onions, carrots, celery, salt, and pepper. Cook over medium-high heat, stirring, until the vegetables are softened, 7 to 8 minutes. Be sure the vegetables do not put on color.

Add the beans, thyme, bay leaf, and 10 cups (2.4 L) water. Bring to a boil, then reduce the heat so the soup is at a simmer, and cook until the soup is flavorful, about 20 minutes. Stir in the escarole and the chorizo and cook until the escarole is wilted, another 10 minutes.

Remove from the heat and discard the thyme sprigs (the leaves will have come off into the soup) and the bay leaf. Ladle the soup into bowls, garnish with the cilantro and scallions, and serve immediately.

PESTO CHICKEN SOUP

SERVES 6

We were inspired by a French soup called *soupe au pistou*, traditionally made with a variety of vegetables and accompanied by a *pistou*, or pesto. Instead of vegetables, however, we decided to pair the pesto with classic chicken soup, and it just might be our favorite soup when we're feeling under the weather. We like to use roasted chicken meat in our version for that extra bit of flavor; if you've got any remaining roasted chicken (see page 181) left over, this soup is a great way to use it. Or you can just buy a rotisserie chicken at your local store and it will work beautifully. Of course, if you have a go-to chicken soup recipe, by all means make it—adding the pesto will reinvigorate a homey classic!

1	tablespoon extra-virgin olive oil
4	cups (500 g) diced onions
2	cups (280 g) diced carrots
2	cups (200 g) diced celery
2	tablespoons kosher salt
½	teaspoon freshly ground black pepper
24	ounces (680 g) cooked and pulled whole chicken
½	bunch thyme sprigs
1	bay leaf
1	cup (240 ml) Pesto (page 47) or store-bought

In a large heavy-bottomed pot, heat the oil over medium heat. Add the onions, carrots, celery, salt, and pepper. Cook, stirring, until the vegetables soften, 7 to 8 minutes. Make sure the vegetables do not put on color.

Add the chicken, thyme, bay leaf, and 6 cups (1.4 L) water. Bring to a boil, lower the heat so the soup is at a simmer, and cook until the soup is flavorful, about 30 minutes. Remove from the heat and discard the thyme sprigs (the leaves will have come off into the soup) and bay leaf.

Ladle the soup into bowls and top each with a spoonful of pesto. Serve immediately.

SPICY KALE SOUP

SERVES 6

Kale is great in soups, as it stands up well to heat, doesn't fall apart, and I just love how hardy and almost meaty it is. Paired with the heat of our Calabrian Chile Sauce (page 57), this soup will make you want to have another spoonful—and another one. Though I live in South Florida, and we don't get cold days often, this is the perfect soup to make when the temperatures start to drop.

1½	teaspoons extra-virgin olive oil
4	cups (500 g) diced onions
2	cups (280 g) diced carrots
2	cups (200 g) diced celery
2	tablespoons kosher salt
½	teaspoon freshly ground black pepper
8	cups (520 g) chopped kale
1	cup (240 ml) Calabrian Chile Sauce (page 57), or to taste
½	bunch thyme sprigs
1	bay leaf
2	tablespoons red wine vinegar

In a large heavy-bottomed pot, heat the oil over medium heat. Add the onions, carrots, celery, salt, and pepper, and cook, stirring, until the vegetables soften, 7 to 8 minutes. Make sure the vegetables do not put on color.

Add the kale, chile sauce, thyme, bay leaf, and red wine vinegar and 6 cups (1.4 L) water. Bring the soup to a boil, then reduce the heat to low, so the soup is at a simmer, and cook until the kale has softened and the soup has a rich vegetable flavor with a hint of chiles, 20 to 30 minutes. Remove from the heat and discard the bay leaf. Ladle the soup into bowls and serve immediately.

WARM BRUSSELS SPROUTS

WITH BURRATA, PEARS, PISTACHIOS, AND CREAMY PARMESAN DRESSING SERVES 4

This salad is creamy, satisfying, and filling, and the variety of textures and temperatures checks all the boxes. Sweet, juicy pear lightens and brightens the warm roasted sprouts, which are a nice contrast against the cool burrata. I like to finish this salad with raw pistachios—the untoasted nuts bring just the right amount of crunch to the soft, yielding ingredients.

Extra-virgin olive oil

1 pound (455 g) Brussels sprouts, trimmed and halved if large

Kosher salt

Freshly ground black pepper

1 firm but ripe green pear, halved, cored, and sliced ¼ inch (6 mm) thick

¼ cup (10 g) torn basil leaves

¼ cup (13 g) torn mint leaves

2 tablespoons picked oregano leaves

¼ cup (60 ml) Creamy Parmesan Dressing (recipe follows)

1 (8-ounce/225-g) pouch burrata cheese

2 tablespoons crushed raw pistachios

Flaky sea salt, such as Maldon, for garnishing

Preheat the oven to 425°F (220°C).

Grease a large baking sheet with oil and spread the Brussels sprouts on top (if Brussels sprouts have been cut, place them cut side down). Drizzle with more oil and, using your hands, distribute the oil so the sprouts are well coated. Season with salt and pepper.

Transfer the baking sheet to the oven and roast the sprouts 15 to 20 minutes, until nicely browned. Remove from the oven, then transfer the Brussels sprouts to a large bowl and let cool until just warm to the touch.

Combine the Brussels sprouts with pear, basil, mint, and oregano. Season to taste with salt and pepper, then toss with the dressing until combined. Divide the salad among four plates, and top each serving with a piece of burrata and a sprinkling of pistachios and sea salt before serving.

CREAMY PARMESAN DRESSING

MAKES ABOUT 1¼ CUPS (300 ML)

- ¼ cup (60 ml) red wine vinegar
- 1 large egg yolk
- 1½ teaspoons Worcestershire sauce
- ¾ teaspoon kosher salt, plus more as needed
- ¼ teaspoon freshly ground black pepper, plus more as needed
- 1 cup (240 ml) canola or another neutral oil
- ½ cup (50 g) finely grated Parmigiano-Reggiano cheese

In a container with tall sides (a 1-quart/1-L deli container works great for this), combine the vinegar, egg yolk, Worcestershire, salt, and pepper. Using an immersion blender, puree until smooth. With the blender motor running, slowly drizzle in the oil until completely incorporated; then fold in cheese until combined. Taste and adjust the seasonings if needed, then transfer the dressing to a lidded jar and refrigerate until ready to use. The dressing will keep, refrigerated, for up to 5 days.

ESCAROLE SALAD

WITH LEMON, ANCHOVY, PARMIGIANO-REGGIANO, AND BREADCRUMBS SERVES 4

I don't want to pick favorites, as this is a book filled with recipes I love, but this just might be my favorite salad—I even prefer it to a traditional Caesar salad! Generally speaking, I'm a sucker for escarole; I love its hardy, meaty crunch. Often confused for a relative of romaine lettuce, it's actually botanically closer to chicory, and its flavor leans slightly (pleasantly) to the bitter. For this salad, what you want to use are the paler, closer-to-center escarole leaves, aka the "hearts," and save the outer leaves for another use, such as a pizza topping (see page 85) or grilled for a vegetable side. The remaining dressing is a great to use as a dip for vegetables—I like to make extra and keep it on hand.

2	cups (440 g) 1-inch/2.5-cm pieces escarole
½	cup (120 ml) Anchovy Dressing (recipe follows)
	Kosher salt
	Freshly ground black pepper
½	cup (50 g) finely grated Parmigiano-Reggiano cheese
½	cup (50 g) Seasoned Breadcrumbs (recipe follows)
8	oil-packed anchovies
	Lemon wedges, for serving

In a large bowl, toss the escarole with the dressing until combined; season to taste with salt and pepper. Divide the salad among four bowls and top each with 2 tablespoons Parmigiano, 2 tablespoons breadcrumbs, and two anchovies. Serve with lemon wedges on the side for squeezing.

ANCHOVY DRESSING

MAKES ABOUT 1 CUP (240 ML)

¼	cup (60 ml) red wine vinegar
2	tablespoons fresh lemon juice
1	small shallot, diced
2	oil-packed anchovy fillets
1	large egg yolk
¾	teaspoon kosher salt
⅛	teaspoon freshly ground black pepper
½	cup (120 ml) canola or another neutral oil

In a container with tall sides (a 1-quart/1-L deli container works great for this), combine the vinegar, lemon juice, shallot, anchovies, egg yolk, salt, and pepper. Using an immersion blender, process until the liquid is smooth and emulsified. With the blender motor running, slowly drizzle in the oil and process until the dressing is thoroughly blended. Use immediately or cover and refrigerate until needed. The dressing will keep, refrigerated, for up to 5 days.

SEASONED BREADCRUMBS

MAKES ABOUT ½ CUP (50 G)

1	tablespoon (15 g) unsalted butter
1½	teaspoons extra-virgin olive oil
1	small garlic clove, minced
½	cup (50 g) breadcrumbs
1½	teaspoons chopped flat-leaf parsley
¾	teaspoon kosher salt
	Pinch freshly ground black pepper

Preheat the oven to 300°F (150°C).

In a small sauté pan, warm the butter and oil over low heat until the butter is melted and foaming. Add the garlic and cook, stirring, about 1 minute, until the garlic is fragrant but doesn't put on any color. Remove from the heat and immediately transfer to a bowl—this ensures that the garlic does not continue to cook.

Meanwhile, in a separate bowl, combine the breadcrumbs, parsley, salt, and pepper. Add the butter-oil-garlic mixture to the breadcrumb mixture and stir until combined. Transfer the buttery breadcrumbs to a parchment paper–lined baking sheet and bake in the oven, stirring midway, for about 10 minutes, until deep golden-brown. Turn the oven off and let the breadcrumbs sit in the oven for about 15 minutes. Transfer to a cooling rack and let cool completely. Use immediately or transfer to a lidded container and store in a cool, dark place for up to 1 week.

CHOPPED SALAD SERVES 4

I believe that a good chopped salad must be packed with lots of different ingredients, flavors, and textures. Most importantly, though, everything in a chopped salad should be small enough to eat with a spoon.

- 1 cup (200 g) uncooked farro
- 8 cups (440 g) packed chopped romaine lettuce
- 1 cup (140 g) finely diced Trugole, Asiago fresco, or Pecorino fresco cheese
- ½ cup (70 g) finely diced carrot
- ¼ cup (35 g) finely diced red onion
- 2 small tomatoes, preferably heirloom, chopped small

- ½ cup (90 g) canned white beans, rinsed and drained
- 1 medium fennel bulb, finely diced
- ½ cup (75 g) quartered Kalamata olives
- ½ cup (120 ml) Creamy Lemon Dressing (recipe follows), plus more as needed
- Kosher salt
- Freshly ground black pepper

In a large pot, bring salted water to boil and cook the farro according to the packet instructions until soft and almost split open. If any water remains, drain it and set the farro aside to cool completely. If not using right away, transfer to a container with a lid, and refrigerate for up to 5 days.

In a large bowl, mix together the farro, lettuce, cheese, carrot, onion, tomatoes, beans, fennel, and olives until combined. Toss with the dressing and season to taste with the salt and pepper. Divide among four bowls and serve.

CREAMY LEMON DRESSING

MAKES ABOUT 1 CUP (240 ML)

- ½ cup plus 2 tablespoons (150 ml) My Favorite Mayonnaise (page 53) or store-bought
- ½ cup (120 ml) fresh lemon juice
- 2 tablespoons diced yellow onion
- 1½ teaspoons mild honey
- 1½ teaspoons Dijon mustard
- 1½ teaspoons thyme leaves
- 1½ teaspoons champagne vinegar
- ¾ teaspoon kosher salt
- Pinch freshly ground black pepper
- ½ cup (120 ml) canola or another neutral oil

In a bowl, combine the mayonnaise, lemon juice, onion, honey, mustard, thyme, vinegar, salt, and pepper. Using an immersion blender, blend for 30 seconds until combined. With the motor running, drizzle in the oil and process until the dressing is completely emulsified. Set aside, or cover and refrigerate for up to 4 days.

ORANGE AND RADISH SALAD

WITH BITTER GREENS, SHAVED FENNEL, GREEN OLIVES, AND PARMIGIANO-REGGIANO SERVES 4

This salad goes well with just about anything. Basically the kind of salad I always want to eat: briny, bright, sweet, tart, crunchy, and salty, it's also beautiful to look at, and features some of my favorite ingredients, like citrus, olives, and a hard, salty cheese.

2	oranges, peel and pith removed
6	cups (180 g) packed mix of bitter greens, such as Belgian endive, radicchio, and arugula
1½	cups (135 g) thinly shaved fennel bulb
1½	cups (175 g) sliced radishes
½	cup (75 g) Castelvetrano olives, pitted and halved
1	Grilled Red Onion (page 56)
⅓	cup (75 ml) Lemon Vinaigrette (recipe follows)
	Wedge of Parmigiano-Reggiano cheese, for serving

Using a paring knife, cut the oranges into sections by carving between the membranes. Place the oranges in a large bowl and add the greens, fennel, radishes, olives, onion, and vinaigrette and toss until combined. Divide the salad among the plates. Using a vegetable peeler, shave strips of Parmigiano, and garnish the salad. Serve immediately.

LEMON VINAIGRETTE

MAKES A GENEROUS 1⅓ CUPS

(315 ML)

1	cup (240 ml) extra-virgin olive oil
⅓	cup plus 1 tablespoon (90 ml) fresh lemon juice, strained

Combine the oil and lemon juice in a jar large enough to hold both liquids, cover tightly, and shake until the dressing is combined and uniform. Cover and set aside or refrigerate until ready to use. This makes more dressing than you need, but it's always good to have extra dressing on hand. The lemon vinaigrette will keep, refrigerated, for up to 5 days.

TOMATOES AND BURRATA

SERVES 4

Featuring a recipe like this is important, because it serves as a stark reminder that good ingredients, treated simply and respectfully, shine on their own and produce a superlative result, which surpasses the individual ingredients on their own. Don't overdo it; don't put anything extra on it.

When you're serving tomatoes and burrata, each ingredient should be at its best, or just make something else. These ingredients, laid bare, leave nothing to hide behind, so if the tomatoes aren't at their most excellent or the burrata is just so-so, this plate won't sing. Just a pinch of flaky sea salt, some freshly cracked black pepper, a basil leaf, and a drizzle of your favorite olive oil, and that's it—magic.

1	(8-ounce/225-g) burrata cheese ball, halved (see Note)
2	large tomatoes, preferably heirloom and at the height of the season, sliced ¼ inch (6 mm) thick
	Handful basil leaves, torn
	Flaky sea salt, such as Maldon
	Freshly ground black pepper
	Extra-virgin olive oil

On a large plate, arrange the burrata and tomatoes. Scatter the basil leaves on top, season with salt and pepper, and drizzle with oil. Serve immediately.

Note: Burrata needs to rest at room temperature for at least 30 minutes to become super creamy.

CELERY ROOT

WITH PECORINO-ROMANO, ARUGULA, AND ALMONDS SERVES 4

Besides *celeri remoulade*, celery root gets little to no spotlight. And that's a shame, because it's such a glorious vegetable and can really hold its own if you just let it. Filled with love for this homely looking root, I wanted to create a salad to celebrate it and imbue it with all the brightness you need when the winter doldrums hit. When you can't buy a ticket to somewhere warm, this can be your little ray of sunshine. When shopping for celery root, make sure the top center is very firm when pressed down; if it has even the slightest give, the celery root is past its prime and won't be as crunchy or refreshing.

¼ cup (60 ml) Lemon Vinaigrette (page 172)

2 teaspoons Calabrian Chile Sauce (page 57), plus more as needed

2 cups (40 g) arugula

½ medium celery root (about 12 ounces/ 340 g), peeled and cut into 2 by ¼-inch matchstick strips

Kosher salt

¼ cup (30 g) chopped toasted almonds

Shavings Parmigiano-Reggiano cheese, for garnishing

To make the dressing, in a small bowl, whisk together the vinaigrette and chile sauce until combined.

In a large bowl, combine the arugula and celery root, add the dressing, and toss until the dressing is evenly distributed. Season to taste with salt and toss again.

Divide the salad among four plates and top with the almonds and Parmigiano shavings. Serve immediately.

KALE SALAD

WITH ROASTED BEETS, ONION, GOAT CHEESE, SUNFLOWER SEED DRESSING, AND DILL SERVES 4

The dark-horse ingredient in this salad is dill; while beets and dill are often paired, kale and dill are not. If you're still on the fence about eating raw kale, this salad just might convince you how delicious it can be. Dressed with a creamy sunflower seed dressing, this salad can easily be a meal all its own, plus the dressing recipe makes more than you need, so you can make more salad in the days to come, or use it as dip for vegetables (raw or roasted!), French fries, chicken, or fish, or as a sandwich spread.

1	large beet, trimmed and scrubbed
8	cups (520 g) rough-chopped Tuscan kale
½	small red onion, thinly sliced
⅓	cup (17 g) chopped dill, plus more for garnishing
2	tablespoons hulled raw sunflower seeds, plus more for garnishing
¼	cup (60 ml) Sunflower Seed Dressing (recipe follows)
	Kosher salt
	Freshly ground black pepper
8	tablespoons (4 ounces/113 g) crumbled goat cheese

Preheat the oven to 425°F (220°C). Wrap the beet in aluminum foil and place on a baking sheet.

Bake the beet for 1 hour to 1 hour 30 minutes, until soft when pierced with a knife. Transfer to a plate and let cool completely before peeling and cutting into large dice.

In a large bowl, combine the beet, kale, onion, dill, and sunflower seeds. Toss with the dressing until the ingredients are coated, and season to taste with salt and pepper. Divide the salad among four plates, garnish with dill and sunflower seeds, and top with the goat cheese before serving.

SUNFLOWER SEED DRESSING

MAKES ABOUT 1¼ CUPS (300 ML)

½	cup (70 g) hulled raw sunflower seeds
½	cup (25 g) packed dill
¼	cup (60 ml) fresh lemon juice
1	teaspoon tahini
¾	teaspoon kosher salt, plus more as needed
¾	teaspoon ground cumin
¼	teaspoon freshly ground black pepper, plus more as needed
½	cup (120 ml) extra-virgin olive oil

In a large bowl, combine the sunflower seeds, dill, lemon juice, tahini, salt, cumin, and pepper with ¼ cup (60 ml) water. Using an immersion blender, process until smooth. With the blender motor running, slowly drizzle in the oil and process until the dressing is emulsified. Taste and adjust the seasonings as needed. Use immediately or cover and refrigerate until ready to use. The dressing will keep, refrigerated, for up to 5 days.

ROASTED CHICKEN

WITH SALSA VERDE AND FENNEL SLAW

SERVES 4

My mantra when roasting a chicken is: Keep it simple. There must be a thousand methods for making it, and ours is one of the more straightforward ones. No need to rub the chicken with oil, truss, slide herbs under the skin, or stuff lemon in the cavity. Here's my secret: Get a good, organic, air-chilled chicken, preferably one that enjoyed a good deal of its life outdoors. Generously season it with salt and pepper, and roast at a high temperature. And that's it! You will get the tastiest, crispiest skin, and if you're left with any rendered fat (aka schmaltz, aka liquid gold), save it for roasting vegetables or frying eggs. Pro tip: If you have any leftover chicken, eat the skin before you put the chicken in the refrigerator—that way you get the crispy skin before it gets soft and mushy.

I like to pair my roasted chicken with something crunchy and bright, like a fennel slaw—tossed while the chicken rests before carving—and a bright herb salsa verde. Together, they transform something known and predictable into a delightful surprise brimming with flavor in every bite. Extra salsa verde makes a great addition to any sandwich.

1   (3½- to 4-pound/1.6- to 1.8-kg) chicken, at room temperature

Kosher salt

Freshly ground black pepper

1   large fennel bulb, trimmed and sliced paper-thin

¼   medium red onion, sliced paper-thin

4   to 5 watermelon radishes or regular radishes, sliced paper-thin

2   navel oranges, peel and pith removed, cut into sections

Handful flat-leaf parsley leaves, chopped

2   tablespoons fresh lemon juice

2   tablespoons extra-virgin olive oil

¼   cup (60 ml) Salsa Verde (recipe follows)

Preheat the oven to 450°F (230°C). Using paper towels, thoroughly pat the chicken dry. Season generously with salt and pepper. If you're worried about over-seasoning, you are probably getting it right—the chicken can take it.

Transfer the chicken to a roasting pan fitted with a rack, and place the pan in the oven. Roast the chicken until it is deep golden-brown and the internal temperature (when you stick a meat thermometer in the thickest part of the thigh) reaches 165°F (74°C), about 1 hour.

Transfer the chicken to a carving board with a groove to catch the juices, and let the chicken sit undisturbed, 15 minutes.

While the chicken is resting, in a large bowl, toss together the fennel, onion, radishes, oranges, and parsley. In a small bowl, whisk together the lemon juice and oil until combined. Just before serving the chicken, toss the dressing with the salad vegetables and season with salt and pepper, if desired.

Carve the chicken into four pieces and divide among the plates. Spoon some salsa verde on top of the chicken. Divide the fennel salad among the plates and serve immediately.

SALSA VERDE

MAKES ABOUT 1 CUP (240 ML)

- ½ bunch flat-leaf parsley, stemmed
- 1½ tablespoons thyme leaves
- 1½ tablespoons capers, drained and roughly chopped
- 1 garlic clove, minced
- 1½ oil-packed anchovies, drained and minced
- ¼ teaspoon dried oregano
- ¼ teaspoon finely grated lemon zest
- ½ cup (120 ml) extra-virgin olive oil

Finely chop the parsley and thyme together. In a bowl, toss together the parsley, thyme, capers, garlic, anchovies, oregano, and lemon zest. Add the oil and stir to combine. Cover and refrigerate until needed. The salsa verde will keep, refrigerated, for up to 3 days.

PAN-ROASTED SKIRT STEAK

WITH FINGERLING POTATOES, ROSEMARY, AND PEPERONATA SERVES 4

This is our stepped-up version of meat and potatoes. We spruce up an otherwise straightforward idea with some *peperonata*, a tart, vinegary bell pepper stew. And while the steak and potatoes offer traditional, familiar flavors, the peperonata, breaking through the fattiness of the meat, livens it up and brings something a little unexpected. Extra peperonata makes for a great addition to sandwiches, or on pizza (see page 134), or served alongside olives and crackers for an *aperitivo* at just the right time.

1	pound (455 g) fingerling or baby potatoes
2	tablespoons extra-virgin olive oil
2	teaspoons rosemary leaves, plus more for garnishing
2	teaspoons kosher salt, plus more as needed
½	teaspoon freshly ground black pepper
1	pound (455 g) skirt steak
2	tablespoons (30 g) unsalted butter ¼ cup (60 ml) Peperonata (recipe follows)
	A sprig of rosemary, for garnishing

Preheat the oven to 425°F (220°C).

Toss the potatoes with 1 tablespoon oil, the rosemary, 2 teaspoons salt, and the pepper, then toss again to distribute. Arrange the potatoes in a single layer, cut side down, on a baking sheet, making sure there is room between the potatoes, and place in the oven.

Roast the potatoes for 20 minutes, or until they are nicely browned and can be easily pierced with a fork. Remove from the oven and set aside.

While the potatoes roast, liberally season the steak on both sides with salt and pepper. Set a cast-iron pan over medium-high heat, and when the pan is hot, add 1 tablespoon oil, rolling it to coat the bottom of the pan. Place the steak in the pan and sear on one side, 5 to 7 minutes, until nicely browned. Flip the steak, add 2 tablespoons (30 g) butter, and transfer the pan to the oven.

Pan-roast the steak until medium-rare and the internal temperature ranges between 130°F and 135°F (54°C and 57°C), 7 to 8 minutes. Immediately remove from the oven and let sit on a cutting board, 10 minutes.

While the steak and potatoes rest, heat the peperonata in the cast-iron pan over medium heat until warm, about 8 minutes.

When ready to serve, cut the steak against the grain and divide among four plates. Divide the potatoes as well and top the steak slices with peperonata. Garnish with rosemary and serve immediately.

PEPERONATA

MAKES ABOUT 4 CUPS (1 LITER)

⅔ cup (165 ml) extra-virgin olive oil

2 large red bell peppers, seeded and sliced into thin strips

4 large garlic cloves, thinly sliced

¾ teaspoon kosher salt, plus more as needed

2 medium yellow onions, halved and thinly sliced

½ teaspoon crushed red pepper, plus more as needed

½ teaspoon freshly ground black pepper, plus more as needed

⅔ cup (165 ml) Marinara (page 45)

⅔ cup (165 ml) red wine vinegar

In a large saucepan, warm the oil over medium heat until shimmering. Add the red bell peppers, garlic, and salt. Cook, stirring, until the vegetables soften, about 15 minutes; don't let the vegetables put on any color.

Add the onions and cook, stirring, for 10 to 15 minutes, until the onions are soft. Stir in the crushed red pepper and black pepper and cook, stirring, for 30 seconds. Add the vinegar and marinara and cook at a mild simmer, stirring from time to time, until the peppers and onions have completely collapsed and the vinegar's acidic bite has considerably mellowed, 10 to 15 minutes. Remove from the heat and serve immediately, or transfer to a container with a lid and refrigerate until needed, for up to 1 week.

ROASTED EGGPLANT

WITH STEWED TOMATOES, FARRO GREMOLATA, AND FETA   SERVES 4

Eggplant as a main course makes for a great meatless dish—tasty and satisfying, and beloved by vegetarians and carnivores alike. We serve it in a pool of warm marinara with nutty, chewy farro and cool, creamy feta, so that every forkful offers contrasting temperatures and flavors.

2	tablespoons extra-virgin olive oil, plus more for greasing the sheet
1	tablespoon red wine vinegar
1	tablespoon chopped rosemary leaves
1	tablespoon honey
1	tablespoon kosher salt
½	teaspoon freshly ground black pepper
1	(2 ½-pound/1.2-kg) Italian eggplant, halved and sliced ½ inch (12 mm) thick
2	cups (480 ml) Marinara (page 45) or store-bought
1	cup (150 g) Farro Gremolata (recipe follows)
¼	cup (40 g) crumbled feta cheese

Preheat the oven to 400°F (205°C). Lightly grease two large baking sheets with oil. In a small bowl, whisk together 2 tablespoons oil with the vinegar, rosemary, honey, salt, and pepper to combine.

In a large bowl, toss the marinade together with the eggplant until evenly distributed. Spread the dressed eggplant in a single layer on the greased baking sheets, making sure it has some breathing room, and roast for 30 minutes, rotating the pans midway through, back to front and up to down, until the eggplant is soft and nicely browned.

While the eggplant is roasting, in a medium saucepan, warm the marinara over medium heat until slightly simmering.

When ready to serve, divide the marinara among four plates. Place the eggplant on top and divide the farro gremolata over the eggplant. Sprinkle with the feta and serve immediately.

FARRO GREMOLATA

MAKES ABOUT 2 CUPS (285 G)

- 2 cups (260 g) cooked farro (see page 171)
- 1 cup (50 g) chopped fresh flat-leaf parsley
- 1½ teaspoons extra-virgin olive oil

  Finely grated zest of 1 lemon
- ½ teaspoon kosher salt, plus more as needed
- ¼ teaspoon freshly ground black pepper, plus more as needed

In a large bowl, combine the farro, parsley, oil, lemon zest, salt, and pepper and mix thoroughly. Set aside. If not using right away, cover and refrigerate for up to 3 days.

MAHI-MAHI

WITH TOMATO, KALE, FENNEL, AND LEMON AIOLI SERVES 4

This fish stew comes together quickly and makes for a delicious weeknight dinner. I love using mahi-mahi, because it's relatively affordable and easy to work with. Local to Florida, mahi-mahi can also be easily found across the country. If you're left with extra onion and fennel stew, you can bake eggs in it for a delicious breakfast. You'll also have extra aioli on hand—it makes a great vegetable dip.

For the onion and fennel stew:

- ¼ cup (60 ml) extra-virgin olive oil, plus more as needed
- 3 garlic cloves, sliced
- 2 teaspoons kosher salt, plus more as needed
- 2 medium yellow onions, halved and sliced thin
- 2 cups (110 g) chopped kale
- 1 fennel bulb, sliced thin
- 1½ teaspoons ground fennel seed
- ¼ teaspoon crushed red pepper
- ¼ teaspoon freshly ground black pepper, plus more as needed
- ½ cup (120 ml) white wine
- 2 cups (480 ml) Marinara (page 45)
- 1 tablespoon drained capers

For the fish:

- 4 (6- to 7-ounce/170- to 200-g) pieces mahi-mahi, patted dry
- ¼ cup (60 ml) Lemon Aioli (recipe follows)

  Arugula leaves, for garnishing

Make the onion and fennel stew:
In a large pan, warm the oil over medium heat until shimmering. Add the garlic and 2 teaspoons salt and cook, stirring, until the garlic is fragrant and softens, about 2 minutes. Make sure the garlic does not put on color.

Add the onions, kale, and fennel bulb and continue to cook, stirring, until the vegetables are translucent and softer, 8 to 10 minutes. Make sure the onions and fennel do not put on color.

Add the fennel seed, crushed red pepper, and ¼ teaspoon black pepper and cook, stirring, until the spices are toasted, about 30 seconds. Add the wine and deglaze, scraping the bottom of the pot with a wooden spoon. Cook until the wine is reduced by half, about 5 minutes.

Add the marinara and capers along with 1 cup (240 ml) water. Raise the heat to medium-high and bring the mixture to a boil. Reduce the heat to low so the mixture is at a simmer and cook for 15 to 20 minutes, until the mixture is the consistency of stew with some juice. Keep warm.

Make the fish:

Preheat the oven to 400°F (205°C).

In a large ovenproof skillet (a quality nonstick pan works great here), add enough oil to cover the bottom of the pot and heat over high heat until the oil is shimmering.

Season the fish with salt and pepper and place the fish in the pan, flesh side down. Cook the fish for 1 minute, until nicely seared, then flip and transfer the pan to the oven. Roast the fish 5 to 7 minutes, or until cooked through and no longer pink in the center.

To serve, divide the onion and fennel stew among four plates, and place one piece of fish over each stew mound. Spoon a dollop of aioli over the fish and garnish with arugula. Serve immediately.

LEMON AIOLI

MAKES ABOUT 1½ CUPS (360 ML)

½	cup (120 ml) My Favorite Mayonnaise (page 53) or store-bought
½	teaspoon finely grated lemon zest
2	teaspoons fresh lemon juice, plus more as needed
1	small clove garlic, minced
	Pinch kosher salt, plus more as needed

In a large bowl, whisk together the mayonnaise, lemon zest and juice, garlic, and salt until combined. Taste and adjust seasonings, if needed. Refrigerate until needed, for up to 2 days.

SLOW-ROASTED PORK SHOULDER

WITH SOFT POLENTA AND SHAVED CELERY SALAD SERVES 6

This is the kind of thing you cook on a cold Sunday afternoon when you're not rushed. Prep the meat the night before to get it ready for the morning. To get extraordinary roasted pork, you cannot rush the process. Pairing the rich, tender meat with some creamy polenta and crunchy shaved celery lightens the pork and makes for a delicious, balanced meal.

For the pork:

- ½ cup (145 g) fennel seeds
- 2 tablespoons crushed red pepper
- 2 tablespoons chili powder
- 2 tablespoons ground coriander
- 2 tablespoons ground cinnamon
- ¾ teaspoon kosher salt, plus more as needed
- ½ teaspoon freshly ground black pepper, plus more as needed
- 1 (5-pound/2.3-kg) boneless pork shoulder, patted dry

    Flaky sea salt, such as Maldon, for garnish

For the soft polenta:

- 2 cups (480 ml) whole milk
- 1 teaspoon kosher salt, plus more as needed
- 1 cup (135 g) medium-grind yellow cornmeal (not quick-cooking)

    Freshly ground black pepper (optional)

For the shaved celery salad:

- 6 cups (300 g) shaved celery
- 1 cup (50 g) roughly chopped parsley leaves
- ½ medium red onion, shaved
- 3 tablespoons fresh lemon juice, plus more as needed
- 3 tablespoons extra-virgin olive oil, plus more as needed

    Kosher salt

    Freshly ground black pepper

    Lemon wedges, for serving

Make the pork:

In a spice grinder, grind the fennel seeds and crushed red pepper into a fine powder. In a small container, combine with the chili powder, coriander, cinnamon, ¾ teaspoon salt, and ½ teaspoon pepper. You can store the rub, covered, in a cool, dark spot for up to 3 months.

Liberally season the meat all over with salt and pepper. Distribute the rub all over the meat. Place on a tray and refrigerate, uncovered, overnight.

When ready to cook, preheat the oven to 350°F (175°C).

Place the meat in a heavy-bottomed ovenproof pot (a Dutch oven is perfect) and add ¾ cup (180 ml) water. Cover the pot with parchment paper and place a lid on top. Transfer to the oven and cook for 6 hours, until the meat is very tender and pulls apart easily. Remove from the oven and let the meat cool completely in the cooking liquid.

Make the soft polenta:

In a medium heavy-bottomed saucepan, bring the milk and 3 cups (720 ml) water to a boil over high heat. Add the salt. Pour the polenta slowly into the liquid, stirring with a wire whisk or wooden spoon. Keep stirring as the mixture thickens, 2 to 3 minutes.

Reduce the heat to low, and cook the polenta until creamy, at least 45 minutes, stirring every 10 minutes. If the polenta becomes quite thick, thin it out with ½ cup (120 ml) water, stir thoroughly, and continue cooking. You can add up to 1 cup (240 ml) more water as necessary, to keep the polenta soft enough to stir.

Drop a small dollop onto a plate, let it cool, then taste. The grains should be swollen and taste cooked, not raw. Season the pot with more salt and some freshly ground pepper, if desired.

Make the shaved celery salad:

While the polenta cooks, in a large bowl, combine the celery, parsley, and onion.

In a small bowl, whisk together the lemon juice and oil until combined.

Right before serving, toss the salad ingredients with the dressing and season to taste with salt and pepper.

To serve: When ready to eat, serve the pork shoulder family-style, with cooked polenta shaved celery salad, and on the side. Garnish with a sprinkle of flaky salt.

SLOW-ROASTED SHORT RIBS

WITH SMASHED CANNELLINI BEANS

SERVES 8 TO 10

We slow-roast our short ribs instead of braising them, because I believe it produces a lighter and brighter preparation for what otherwise can be an oppressively rich and heavy dish. I don't want anyone falling asleep after eating it, and that's kind of the feeling I myself often get after eating braised short ribs. Slow-roasting the ribs also makes for more versatile leftovers. You can add the leftover meat to pizza (see page 79) or make the most comforting, satisfying soup (see page 157). Make extra and enjoy the benefits of my "cook once, eat twice (or even three times)" philosophy.

For the ribs:

- 6 tablespoons (12 g) dried porcini mushrooms
- 2 tablespoons plus 1 teaspoon smoked paprika
- 2 tablespoons plus 1 teaspoon kosher salt
- 2 tablespoons plus 1 teaspoon powdered ginger
- 2½ teaspoons chipotle chile powder
- 5 garlic cloves, grated on a Microplane
- 2 tablespoons canola oil
- 6 (1-pound/455-g) bone-in short ribs, rinsed and patted dry
- 1 cup (240 ml) Tomato Sauce (page 44)
- 2 tablespoons extra-virgin olive oil, plus more as needed
- 1 tablespoon red wine vinegar

For the cannellini beans:

- 1½ cups (280 g) dried cannellini beans

  Kosher salt
- 1 cup (50 g) chopped flat-leaf parsley
- ¼ cup (35 g) minced red onion
- 2 garlic cloves, minced

  Finely grated zest of 1 lemon

  Extra-virgin olive oil

Make the ribs:

Place the mushrooms in a spice grinder and process until they are ground to a fine powder. In a medium bowl, combine the ground mushrooms with the paprika, salt, ginger, chipotle chile powder, and garlic until uniform. Add the oil and stir until you get a super-thick paste. (If your paste looks too thick, add more oil, 1 tablespoon at a time.) Distribute all but about a fifth or sixth of the rub all over the ribs (set aside the remaining rub) and refrigerate the ribs, uncovered, overnight or for up to 12 hours.

When ready to cook, remove the ribs from the refrigerator and let them come to room temperature, about 1 hour. Preheat the oven to 400°F (205°C).

Place the ribs, bone side down, on a half-sheet baking pan and transfer to the oven. Roast the meat for 45 minutes to 1 hour, until richly browned.

Remove the ribs from the oven and lower the oven temperature to 325°F (165°C). Add ½ cup (120 ml) water to the pan. Cover the pan with heavy-duty aluminum foil to seal in the moisture. Return the ribs to the oven and roast for 3 hours, or until the meat is tender and falling off the bone.

Right before serving, combine the reserved rub with the tomato sauce, oil, and vinegar until uniform. Set the sauce aside.

Make the cannellini beans:

While the ribs cure overnight, soak the beans in plenty of cold water for at least 5 hours, preferably overnight.

After soaking, drain and rinse the beans, then transfer them to a large pan, cover with 2 inches (5 cm) cold water, and bring to a boil over medium-high heat. Scoop off any gray scum that forms, then reduce the heat to low, so the water is at a simmer, and cook until the beans are tender, 1 hour to 1 hour 30 minutes. Keep an eye on the water amount, and add more if necessary.

When the beans are tender, season to taste with salt, and remove from the heat. Spoon half of the beans into a bowl. Mash the remaining beans and then stir in the reserved whole beans. Add the parsley, onion, garlic, and lemon zest, and mix to combine. Finish with a good dousing of oil.

To serve, present the ribs and the beans family-style, so everyone can help himself or herself. Serve the tomato sauce on the side, and drizzle it over the meat before eating.

MERGUEZ MEATBALLS

WITH CRUNCHY SALAD AND HERBED YOGURT SERVES 4

Merguez is Middle Eastern sausage made with ground lamb, herbs, and spices. You can buy it in stores, but it's also incredibly easy to make at home. And while many consider lamb to be heavy, this is a dish that doesn't weigh you down. Brightened by a crunchy salad and a tart herbed yogurt, it tastes lively and light. Save a little piece of uncooked merguez to make pizza the following day—and see just how versatile this sausage is.

For the merguez:

- ½ teaspoon cumin seeds
- ½ teaspoon coriander seeds
- ½ teaspoon fennel seeds
- 1 pound (455 g) ground lamb
- 2 tablespoons finely chopped cilantro, plus more for garnishing
- 2 garlic cloves, minced
- 1½ teaspoons kosher salt
- 1 teaspoon paprika
- ½ teaspoon cayenne pepper, or to taste

For the herbed yogurt:

- 1 cup (240 ml) plain strained or Greek yogurt
- 2 teaspoons chopped cilantro
- 2 teaspoons chopped mint
- 2 teaspoons chopped dill
- 2 teaspoons harissa
- 1 tablespoon finely chopped Preserved Lemons (page 63), rind and flesh
- 2 teaspoons brine from Preserved Lemons (page 63), plus more as needed

For the crunchy salad:

- 4 cups (80 g) arugula
- 1 cup (145 g) halved cherry tomatoes
- 2 Persian cucumbers, halved lengthwise and sliced
- 2 to 3 radishes, thinly sliced
- ¼ medium red onion, thinly sliced
- Large handful mixed herbs, such as parsley, mint, cilantro, and dill
- ¼ cup (60 ml) Lemon Vinaigrette (page 172), plus more as needed
- Kosher salt
- Freshly ground black pepper

For serving:

- Flaky sea salt, such as Maldon
- Pita (optional; see Note, page 201)

Make the merguez:

In a small pan, toast the cumin, coriander, and fennel seeds over medium-low heat until fragrant, 1 to 2 minutes. Transfer the seeds to a spice grinder or a mortar, and process until finely ground.

In a large bowl, combine the ground spices with the lamb, cilantro, garlic, salt, paprika, and cayenne and mix with your hands until thoroughly incorporated. Form the mixture into golf ball–size meatballs and place on a shallow baking sheet. Refrigerate for at least 30 minutes before cooking. If not using right away, the meatballs can be covered and refrigerated for up to 4 days, or frozen for up to 3 months. (If planning to make the Merguez Pizza on page 125, set aside 1 to 2 uncooked meatballs for that purpose.)

While the meatballs are in the refrigerator, preheat the oven to 425°F (220°C). Roast the meatballs until cooked through and the centers are no longer pink, about 12 minutes. Remove from the oven and serve immediately.

Make the herbed yogurt sauce:

While the merguez cooks, in a 1-quart (1-L) deli container, stir together the yogurt, cilantro, mint, dill, harissa, and preserved lemon rind and flesh until combined.

Add 2 teaspoons preserved lemon brine. Using an immersion blender, process the mixture until smooth and only the tiniest green flecks remain. If the sauce needs to be looser, add another teaspoon of the brine and blend to combine. Set aside. If not serving immediately, cover and refrigerate for up to 2 days.

Make the crunchy salad:

In a large bowl, toss together the arugula, tomatoes, cucumbers, radishes, onion, and herbs until combined. Right before serving, dress with the vinaigrette and season to taste with salt and pepper.

To serve, spread the yogurt sauce on four plates, then arrange the meatballs and salad on top. Garnish with a pinch of flaky salt.

If you like, you can stuff the salad, the meatballs (slightly flatten them first), and the sauce into pitas, and enjoy as a sandwich.

____

Note: You can also make homemade pita using Pizza Dough (page 31). Place a pizza stone or baking sheet inside the oven and heat the oven to 500°F (260°C) for at least 30 minutes before baking. Roll out an 8-ounce (225-g) ball of dough to an 8-inch (20-cm) circle. Place the dough on the hot pizza stone or baking sheet and bake for 3 to 4 minutes, until puffed and golden brown.

■

BUTTERMILK PANNA COTTA

WITH COMPOTE

SERVES 6

I love a good panna cotta, but it's easy to get carried away—if you don't want the results to appear bulletproof, go easy on the gelatin when you're giving this panna cotta a whirl. It's perfect for your next dinner party: Make it in advance, and then look effortlessly cool while serving your guests dessert without breaking a sweat. Pair it with your favorite fruit compote, or offer a selection. (I suggest blueberry, orange anise, peach, sour cherry, and strawberry-basil; see pages 204–205.) And having extra is never a problem; the compotes are also delicious on vanilla ice cream or spread on toast.

1	cup (240 ml) heavy cream
½	cup (100 g) granulated sugar
¾	teaspoon kosher salt
¼	vanilla bean, split and scraped
2	sheets gelatin or 2 teaspoons powdered gelatin
2	cups (480 ml) well-shaken buttermilk
	Ice, for ice bath
	Fruit compote of your choice (recipes follow)

In a medium heavy-bottomed pot, combine the cream, sugar, salt, and vanilla bean and seeds. Slowly bring the mixture to a simmer over medium heat, whisking to dissolve the sugar and salt completely.

Meanwhile, if using gelatin sheets, soak them in a small bowl of ice water for 2 minutes or until soft—this is called "blooming." Remove the sheets from the water, squeeze out any extra water, and set aside. If using powdered gelatin, put it in a small bowl with 1 tablespoon cold water and let it soak for 5 minutes or until soft. In a medium bowl, prepare an ice bath.

Add the buttermilk to the cream mixture. When the buttermilk mixture comes to a simmer, remove it from the heat and whisk in the gelatin sheets or powdered gelatin until dissolved. Pour the mixture into a bowl set over an ice bath and stir until very cold, about 5 minutes.

Ladle the mixture into six 4-ounce (120-ml) ramekins or glasses. Cover them with plastic wrap and refrigerate for at least 6 hours, or up to 1 week. If you would prefer not to serve them in the ramekins, unmold them by running a paring knife around the inside rim of each ramekin, then turn upside down over a serving plate to release the panna cotta. Otherwise, serve as is, along with the fruit compote of your choosing.

BLUEBERRY COMPOTE

MAKES ABOUT 3 CUPS (720 ML)

6	cups (870 g) fresh blueberries or 6 cups (930 g) frozen blueberries
1	sprig rosemary
2	tablespoons red wine vinegar
½	cup (100 g) sugar
1½	teaspoons vanilla extract
	Pinch kosher salt

In a large heavy-bottomed pot, combine the blueberries, rosemary, vinegar, sugar, vanilla, and salt with ½ cup (120 ml) water and bring to a simmer over medium heat, stirring occasionally. Cook, uncovered and stirring occasionally, until the mixture thickens to the consistency of syrup, 15 to 20 minutes. Remove from the heat and set aside to cool completely. Use immediately, or cover and refrigerate for up to 2 weeks.

PEACH COMPOTE

MAKES ABOUT 3 CUPS (720 ML)

2	pounds (910 g) small to medium peaches, about 8
	Ice, for ice bath
½	cup (100 g) sugar
¼	cup (60 ml) champagne vinegar
2	thyme sprigs
1	teaspoon kosher salt
½	vanilla bean, split and scraped
	Finely grated zest and juice of 1 lemon

Bring a large pot of water to a boil. While the water heats, make a small "x" incision on the bottom of each peach (not the stem end). In a large bowl, prepare an ice bath.

Gently lower the peaches into the boiling water and blanch them for 2 minutes. Remove the peaches from the water using a spider, and transfer them to the prepared ice bath. Let them cool, then peel, halve, and pit the peaches. Using your hands, crush the peach halves into smallish chunks and place in a large heavy-bottomed pot.

Add the sugar, vinegar, thyme, salt, vanilla bean and seeds, and lemon zest and juice. Bring the mixture to a simmer over medium heat. Cook, uncovered, stirring from time to time, until the mixture thickens to the consistency of syrup, 15 to 20 minutes. Remove from the heat, discard the vanilla pod and thyme, and set the compote aside to cool completely. Use immediately, or cover and refrigerate for up to 5 days.

SOUR CHERRY COMPOTE

MAKES ABOUT 1 QUART (960 ML)

1¼	pounds (570 g) dried cherries
½	cup (100 g) sugar
2	tablespoons red wine vinegar
½	teaspoon kosher salt

In a large heavy-bottomed pot, combine the cherries, sugar, vinegar, and salt with 1 quart (960 ml) water and bring to a simmer over medium heat, stirring occasionally. Cook, uncovered, stirring occasionally, until the mixture thickens to the consistency of syrup, 15 to 20 minutes. Remove from the heat and set aside to cool completely. Use immediately, or cover and refrigerate for up to 2 weeks.

STRAWBERRY-BASIL COMPOTE

MAKES ABOUT 1 QUART (960 ML)

3	pints (about 2 pounds/910 g strawberries, hulled and chopped
1	cup (200 g) sugar
¼	cup (60 ml) red wine vinegar
½	bunch basil
1½	teaspoons vanilla extract
1	teaspoon kosher salt
	Finely grated zest of ½ lemon

In a large heavy-bottomed pot, combine the strawberries, sugar, vinegar, basil, vanilla, salt, and lemon zest with 1 cup (240 ml) water and bring to a simmer over medium heat, stirring occasionally. Cook, uncovered, stirring occasionally, until the mixture thickens to the consistency of syrup, 15 to 20 minutes. Remove from the heat and set aside to cool completely. Use immediately, or cover and refrigerate for up to 2 weeks.

ORANGE-ANISE COMPOTE

MAKES ABOUT 1½ CUPS (360 ML)

1	large orange
¾	cup (150 g) sugar
¼	cup (60 ml) fresh orange juice, strained
¼	cup (60 ml) champagne vinegar
1	sprig rosemary
¾	teaspoon anise seeds

Slice the ends off the orange, score the peel from one end to the other, and remove the peels from the orange. Slice the peels into thin strips.

Bring water to a boil in a small pot over high heat. Add the peels to the boiling water and blanch them for about 3 minutes. Drain and rinse the peels, and repeat this process two more times. This removes the bitterness from the peels.

In a large heavy-bottomed pot, combine the blanched orange peels with the sugar, orange juice, vinegar, rosemary, anise seeds, and ½ cup (120 ml) water and bring to a simmer over medium heat. Cook, uncovered, stirring occasionally, until the mixture thickens to the consistency of syrup, 15 to 20 minutes. Remove from the heat and set aside to cool completely. Use immediately, or cover and refrigerate for up to 2 weeks.

ZEPPOLE

WITH HONEY-WHIPPED RICOTTA
SERVES 4 TO 6

I don't know anyone who doesn't love freshly fried doughnuts, dusted with powdered sugar and served while hot. What makes our zeppole stand out from the pack is the honey-whipped ricotta we serve alongside. That little bit of honey highlighted by orange zest brings new life to these rustic donuts. Very important: When cutting your zeppole pieces and transporting them to the hot oil (please be careful!), handle the dough as gently as possible, so as not to deflate any air bubbles that have formed.

1   quart (960 ml) canola oil, for frying

1   (8-ounce/225-g) ball Pizza Dough
    (page 31), at room temperature

    Confectioners' sugar, for dusting

½   cup (120 ml) Honey-Whipped Ricotta
    (recipe follows), or more to taste

In a heavy-bottomed medium pot, warm the oil to 375°F (190°C) over medium heat.

While the oil warms, gently, so as not to depress the risen dough, cut the dough ball in half, then cut the half into quarters. Once the oil has reached the right temperature, working in two batches, gently lower the dough pieces into the hot oil, and fry until golden brown and cooked through, 4 to 5 minutes. Transfer the zeppole to a bowl of confectioners' sugar and toss to coat.

Serve immediately with a side of honey-whipped ricotta.

HONEY-WHIPPED RICOTTA
MAKES ABOUT 1 CUP (240 ML)

1   orange

1   cup (240 ml) Homemade
    Ricotta (page 150), or
    store-bought

1½   tablespoons mild honey

Finely zest the orange directly into the bowl of a food processor fitted with a blade (this ensures you keep all the oils to flavor the ricotta), until you have about ¼ teaspoon. Add the ricotta and the honey. Process the mixture for 2 minutes or until completely smooth. The consistency of the ricotta should be thick and coat a spoon when serving. Transfer the whipped ricotta to a container and refrigerate until needed. It will keep, refrigerated, for up to 4 days.

CHERRY AND CHOCOLATE BISCOTTI

MAKES ABOUT 18 LARGE BISCOTTI

The trick to biscotti is baking them twice (*biscotti* in Italian means "cooked twice"). This allows biscotti to be stored almost indefinitely and makes them a terrific candidate for care packages.

	Finely grated zest of 2 oranges
1½	cups (300 g) sugar
2	cups (250 g) all-purpose flour
½	cup (75 g) dried cherries
½	cup (85 g) chopped dark chocolate
1½	teaspoons baking powder
1½	teaspoons kosher salt
2	large egg yolks
1	teaspoon vanilla extract
4	large eggs

Preheat the oven to 350°F (175°C).

In a medium bowl, rub the orange zest and sugar together. In a separate bowl, whisk together the flour, cherries, chocolate, baking powder, and salt until combined. Whisk in the sugar-zest mixture until combined. In a small bowl, combine the egg yolks and vanilla, and set aside.

Using a sturdy silicone spatula or a wooden spoon, add the whole eggs, one by one, to the dry ingredients, followed by the egg yolks, mixing well between each addition. As you stir (it will seem interminable), you will think this dough needs more liquid, but just keep stirring. As you stir, turn the dough over and over, pressing down on it firmly until incorporated.

Wet your hands with cold water—it will prevent the dough from sticking to your hands while you shape the "logs"—and divide the dough in half. Form each half into a log about 7 inches (17 cm) long and 4 inches (10 cm) wide. Place the log on a parchment paper–lined baking sheet and bake for about 30 minutes, reversing the sheet front to back once during baking, until lightly browned.

Remove the logs from the oven and let cool on a wire rack.

Reduce the oven temperature to 300°F (150°C).

Transfer the cooled logs to a cutting board and, using a large serrated knife, slice them into individual biscotti ¾ inch (2 cm) wide. Return the biscotti to the parchment-lined baking sheet and bake until browned and crisp, about 25 minutes. Let cool completely on a wire rack before eating. You can also store these indefinitely in an airtight container at room temperature.

Variation: In place of cherries and chocolate, use 1 cup (140 g) whole raw almonds and 1 tablespoon anise seeds.

DARK CHOCOLATE CREMOSO

WITH CANDIED ORANGE PEEL, SOFT CREAM, AND PINE NUTS SERVES 6

This delicious dessert is another perfect make-ahead treat. Rich, cold chocolate cremoso is made even more decadent by the flavors of orange and a pinch of flaky sea salt. Easy to make—and even easier to eat!

For the cremoso:

- 10 ounces (280 g) dark chocolate (70% is great), finely chopped
- 1⅓ cups (315 ml) heavy cream
- 3 tablespoons granulated sugar
- 3 large egg yolks
- 3 tablespoons toasted pine nuts

For the candied orange peel:

- 2 large oranges, with ¼ inch (6 mm) cut off the top and bottom
- 4 cups (800 g) granulated sugar

For the soft cream:

- 1½ cups (360 ml) heavy cream
- ⅓ cup (35 g) sifted confectioners' sugar
- 1 teaspoon vanilla extract

For serving:

- Extra-virgin olive oil, for drizzling
- Flaky sea salt, such as Maldon
- 1 tablespoon toasted pine nuts

Make the cremoso:

Put the chocolate in a heatproof bowl and set aside. In an ovenproof bowl, combine the cream and sugar. Bring a pot of water to simmer over medium heat and set the ovenproof bowl over it (do not let the bottom of the bowl touch the water). Stir often until the cream mixture is steaming and the sugar is completely dissolved.

While the cream mixture warms, in a bowl, whisk the egg yolks until slightly thick and pale yellow. Whisking constantly, slowly drizzle the hot cream mixture into the egg yolks (this is called tempering)—if you add the hot cream mixture too quickly, the eggs will scramble. Transfer the cream-and-egg-yolk mixture back to the bowl set over simmering water, and whisk nonstop until the custard is thick enough to coat the back of a spoon, about 2 minutes. Do not let the custard boil.

Pour the custard over the chocolate and whisk thoroughly until the chocolate is completely melted and the mixture is smooth. Divide the cremoso mixture among six shallow bowls. Cover and refrigerate the cremoso until completely firm, at least 6 hours or, even better, overnight. The cremoso can be prepared 1 to 2 days in advance.

Make the candied orange peel:

Score the peel on each orange into 4 vertical sections; remove each section (including white pith) in one piece. Cut these into ¼-inch- (6-mm-) wide strips. In a large pot, bring water to a boil over high heat and cook the peels until softened, about 15 minutes. Drain, rinse, and drain again.

In a medium saucepan, bring 3 cups (600 g) of the sugar and 3 cups (720 ml) water to boil over medium heat, stirring to dissolve the sugar. Add the orange peels and return the mixture to a boil. Reduce the heat and let the peels simmer in the syrup until the peels are very soft, about 45 minutes. Drain.

Toss the peels with the remaining 1 cup (200 g) sugar on a rimmed baking sheet, separating strips with your fingers. Once the peels are nicely coated in sugar, transfer them to a parchment-lined tray. Let stand until the sugar is dry, about 24 hours (and up to 48 hours if the air is humid). The candied orange peels, also known as *orangettes*, can be made ahead and frozen for up to 2 months.

Make the soft cream:

Using a handheld mixer, starting with low speed and increasing to high, whip the cream with the confectioners' sugar and vanilla until soft peaks form, about 6 minutes. Cover the cream with plastic wrap and refrigerate for at least 1 hour and up to overnight.

To serve, drizzle each cremoso with oil and sprinkle with sea salt. Divide the pine nuts among the bowls, followed by some candied orange peels and dollops of soft cream.

CHOCOLATE CHUNK COOKIES

MAKES ABOUT 12 LARGE COOKIES

Our former pastry chef, Hedy Goldsmith, came up with this genius idea of stuffing a chunk of chocolate inside a ball of cookie dough and baking it as such (as opposed to mixing chocolate chips into the dough before spooning the cookies out). These cookies are on the thicker side, slightly soft and yielding in the center, and the chocolate is a bit of a surprise, since you don't see it on the outside. Over the years, we've tweaked the recipe slightly and the version below is our favorite one to date. Topping the cookies with flaky salt is, of course, optional, but I think you should absolutely do it— it takes the cookie from great to truly incredible.

2	sticks (1 cup/225 g) cold unsalted butter, cut into several pieces
¾	cup plus 2 tablespoons (175 g) granulated sugar
	Generous ¾ cup (175 g) packed dark brown sugar
2	large eggs, cold
2	teaspoons vanilla extract
3½	cups (405 g) all-purpose flour
1½	teaspoons kosher salt
1½	teaspoons baking soda
12	(1-ounce/30-g) chocolate chunks or 84 chocolate fèves (7 per cookie)
	Flaky sea salt, such as Maldon

Preheat the oven to 350°F (175°F).

In a stand mixer fitted with the paddle attachment, cream the butter, granulated sugar, and brown sugar on medium-high speed until light and fluffy. Add the eggs, one at a time, until fully incorporated. Pause the mixer motor to scrape the sides and bottom of the bowl between each addition. Add the vanilla and mix to incorporate.

In a separate bowl, whisk together the flour, salt, and baking soda until combined.

Add the flour mixture to the butter-egg mixture and mix on low speed until just combined. Do not overmix.

Using a large cookie scoop (2 ounces/55 g), scoop out the dough and place on a parchment-lined baking sheet. Press a chocolate chunk or 7 chocolate fèves into each of the cookie dough balls and wrap the dough around the chocolate so it's completely encased and the dough balls are round. Return the cookies balls to the parchment-lined baking sheet, flatten the cookies so they're a bit squat, and sprinkle each with some flaky salt.

Bake the cookies for 10 to 12 minutes, or until they are golden brown and about ½ inch (12 mm) thick. Remove from the oven and transfer the cookies to a cooling rack. Let cool completely, then transfer to a container with a lid and store the cookies at room temperature for up to 1 week.

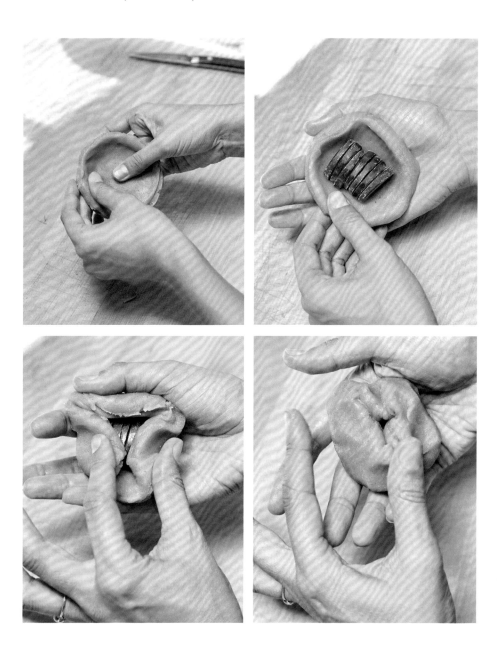

███████

STRAWBERRY-BASIL SODA

MAKES 1 DRINK

The strawberry season in South Florida comes at us fast and furious, and when it arrives, we've got a glut of delicious, ripe berries on our hands—juicy, fragrant, and begging to be used in as many ways as possible. This is one of our homemade sodas, which we created to offer a better-quality, lower-sugar soft drink to our guests.

2	tablespoons Strawberry-Basil Syrup (recipe follows)
1	cup (240 ml) chilled club soda or seltzer
1	strawberry slice, for garnishing

In a tall glass filled with ice, add the syrup and top with the soda. Garnish with a strawberry slice and serve immediately.

STRAWBERRY-BASIL SYRUP

**MAKES ABOUT 1½ CUPS
(360 ML), ENOUGH FOR
12 DRINKS**

½	cup (105 g) demerara sugar
4	cups (660 g) chopped strawberries
10	basil leaves

In a small pot, bring 1 cup (240 ml) water to a boil over high heat. Add the sugar and stir to dissolve. Add the strawberries and bring to a boil. Reduce the heat to low so the mixture is at a simmer, and stir from time to time until the berries fully break down, 10 to 12 minutes. Remove the pot from the heat, stir in the basil, and let the syrup cool to room temperature. Strain the syrup into a nonreactive jar, pressing on the solids. Use immediately, or cover and refrigerate for up to 1 week.

VANILLA-ALLSPICE SODA

MAKES 1 DRINK

Another homemade soda recipe, this is an homage to a classic cream soda, but with real vanilla bean spiked with some fragrant allspice. The resulting syrup is incredibly versatile. For instance, you could use it in a rum-based cocktail that calls for simple syrup; the notes of vanilla and allspice will add a hint of complexity to the drink.

2   tablespoons Vanilla-Allspice Syrup (recipe follows)

1   cup (240 ml) chilled club soda or seltzer

In a glass filled with ice, add the syrup and top with the soda. Serve immediately.

VANILLA-ALLSPICE SYRUP

MAKES ABOUT 1¼ CUPS (300 ML), ENOUGH FOR 10 DRINKS

1   cup (200 g) sugar

1   tablespoon whole allspice berries

½   vanilla bean, split and scraped

In a small pot, bring 1 cup (240 ml) water to a boil over high heat. Add the sugar and stir to dissolve.

Meanwhile, in a small pan, toast the allspice over low heat until fragrant, 5 to 7 minutes. Remove from the heat and immediately transfer the allspice to a bowl to prevent it from burning.

Add the vanilla bean and seeds and the toasted allspice to the syrup, reduce the heat to low, and simmer until the syrup is infused, about 10 minutes. Remove the pot from the heat and let the syrup cool to room temperature. Strain the syrup into a nonreactive jar, pressing on the solids. Use immediately, or cover and refrigerate for up to 1 week.

WATERMELON SPRITZ

This is a refreshing low-alcohol drink perfect for a sweltering day, and a great way to kick off a dinner party. The addition of the two bitters lends some complexity to this fresh and fruity cocktail.

3	ounces (90 ml) fresh watermelon juice
1	ounce (30 ml) Aperol
¾	teaspoon fresh lemon juice
3	ounces (90 ml) prosecco
2	dashes orange bitters
2	dashes lime bitters
1	thin lemon slice, for garnishing

In a wine glass filled with ice cubes, add the watermelon juice, followed by the Aperol and lemon juice. Top with prosecco and float the orange and lime bitters on top. Stir gently and garnish with the lemon slice. Serve immediately.

TORINO SPRITZ

MAKES 1 DRINK

The base of this spritz is Cocchi (pronounced "co-key") Americano vermouth from Torino (Turin), Italy. This is another great effervescent cocktail perfect for kicking the night off. For the James Bond fans out there, Cocchi Americano is the closest you can get to Kina Lillet, the original ingredient in the Vesper cocktail.

3	ounces (90 ml) Cocchi Americano
3	basil leaves
3	ounces (90 ml) chilled club soda
1	lemon wedge

In a wine glass filled with ice, add the Cocchi Americano. Place the basil in one hand, and with your other hand, clap the basil a few times to bruise the leaves. Add the basil to the glass, top with the club soda, then squeeze the lemon into the glass and drop it in the drink. Stir gently and serve immediately.

LEMON-ORANGE SANGRIA

MAKES 1 DRINK

Traditional sangria is typically made with red wine, but we wanted to do something that was lighter, and therefore perfect to drink on a hot summer afternoon. You should use unoaked white wine for this sangria—the oak will make the otherwise light drink taste heavier.

1   (750-ml) bottle unoaked white wine, such as Sauvignon Blanc or Pinot Grigio

¾   cup (180 ml) fresh orange juice, strained

3   tablespoons (45 ml) fresh lemon juice, strained

1   orange, sliced into thin rounds

2   lemons, sliced into thin rounds

In a 1½- to 2-quart (1.5- to 2-L) container, pour in the wine, orange and lemon juices, and orange and lemon slices. Refrigerate until cold, about 2 hours.

When ready to serve, transfer the sangria to a pitcher filled with ice cubes. Pour into wine glasses filled with ice, and use a long spoon to ladle the fruit into the glasses to garnish the drinks.

SHERRY TEMPLE

MAKES 1 DRINK

Obviously a play on a beloved nonalcoholic American drink, the Shirley Temple, our version is spiked with a bit of sherry, another low-alcohol bar staple. Sherry, a fortified wine, marries beautifully here with homemade grenadine, and proves yet again that putting together a few quality ingredients can yield an unbeatable concoction. While you don't need to buy the most expensive sherry out there, don't get the cheapest one, either. Ask a trusted salesperson at your favorite wine shop to suggest a bottle you'll enjoy both drinking and mixing in cocktails.

1 ounce (30 ml) Homemade Grenadine (recipe follows)

¼ cup (60 ml) Fino sherry

3 ounces (90 ml) chilled club soda

1 lime wedge

In a wine glass filled with ice, combine the grenadine and sherry, and top with the soda. Squeeze the lime wedge into the glass and drop it in the drink. Stir and serve immediately.

HOMEMADE GRENADINE

MAKES ABOUT 1½ CUPS
(360 ML), ENOUGH FOR
12 DRINKS

1 cup (200 g) sugar

½ cup (120 ml) pomegranate juice

1 teaspoon pomegranate molasses

1 to 2 dashes orange blossom water

In a small pot, combine the sugar, juice, molasses, and orange blossom water with ½ cup (120 ml) water, and bring to a simmer over medium heat—do not let the liquid boil. Remove from the heat and let cool to room temperature. Use immediately, or cover and refrigerate for up to 1 week.

ITALIAN MICHELADA

MAKES 1 DRINK

The Italian menu long ago coopted the Caesar salad, which, according to lore, was first served in Tijuana, Mexico, making it not 100 percent Italian in origin. Now it's high time for a pizza place to steal a Mexican beverage, as well. Here is that perfect Bloody Mary alternative you didn't realize you've been looking for—savory, spicy, and effervescent. The herbed salt is great to have on hand for anything you wish to add seasoned salt to.

   Herbed Salt (recipe follows)
1   teaspoon Calabrian Chile Sauce (page 57)
¾   teaspoon fresh lime juice
1   (12-ounce/360-ml) bottle Italian lager beer, such as Menabrea Birra Bionda or Peroni
1   lime wedge, for garnishing

Rim half of a chilled glass with the herbed salt. Add the chile sauce and lime juice to the glass, and stir to combine. Gently top with the beer to the glass's brim. Serve immediately.

HERBED SALT

MAKES ABOUT 1 CUP (135 G)

2   tablespoons dried oregano
2   tablespoons dried parsley
2   tablespoons dried thyme
2   tablespoons dried basil
½   cup (120 g) kosher salt

In a bowl, combine the oregano, parsley, thyme, basil, and salt and whisk until combined. Transfer the herbed salt to a clean, dry jar with a lid and store at room temperature for up to 3 months.

We asked some of the folks involved in putting this book together what their ideal menu from Genuine Pizza would look like, and here's what they came up with. You'll see a few repeating dishes, especially those infamous chocolate chunk cookies. We hope they inspire you as you create your perfect menu—centered around pizza, of course!

BRADLEY HERRON
Culinary Director

— Polenta Fries with Spicy Ketchup (page 145)

— Oven-Roasted Chicken Wings with Agrodolce Glaze and Rosemary Crema (page 141)

— Escarole Salad with Lemon, Anchovy, Parmigiano-Reggiano, and Breadcrumbs (page 167)

— Meatball Pizza (page 85)

— Pesto Pizza with Fresh Tomato and Homemade Ricotta (page 93)

— Chocolate Chunk Cookies (page 213)

DILLION WOLFF
Culinary Assistant

— Polenta Fries with Spicy Ketchup (page 145)

— Tomatoes and Burrata (page 175)

— Stracciatella Pizza with Spicy Roasted Tomato Sauce and Scallion (page 111)

— Caponata Pizza (page 76)

— Buttermilk Panna Cotta with Compote (page 202)

MICHAEL SCHWARTZ
Chef and Owner

— Torino Spritz (page 222)

— Tomatoes and Burrata (page 175)

— Bitter Greens Pizza (page 134)

— Roasted Chicken with Salsa Verde and Fennel Slaw (page 181)

— Anise-Almond Biscotti (page 209)

OLGA MASSOV
Coauthor

— Sherry Temple (page 225)

— Caponata with Focaccia (page 147)

— Clam Pizza with Preserved Lemon, Parmigiano-Reggiano, and Mint (page 121)

— Orange and Radish Salad with Bitter Greens, Shaved Fennel, Green Olives, and Parmigiano-Reggiano (page 172)

— Zeppole with Honey-Whipped Ricotta (page 206)

SIDNEY BENSIMON
Photographer

— Lemon-Orange Sangria (page 223)

— Stracciatella Pizza with Spicy Roasted Tomato Sauce and Scallion (page 111)

— Celery Root with Pecorino-Romano, Arugula, and Almonds (page 176)

— Chocolate Chunk Cookies (page 213)

MARTHA BERNABE
Props Mistress

— Marinated Olives (page 153)

— Soppressata Pizza with Mozarella, Calabrian Chile Sauce, and Scallion (page 129)

— Zucchini Pizza (page 131)

— Merguez Meatballs with Crunchy Salad and Herbed Yogurt (page 199)

— Dark Chocolate Cremoso with Candied Orange Peel, Soft Cream, and Pine Nuts (page 210)

JACKIE SAYET
Senior Director, Brand and Culture

— Torino Spritz (page 222)

— Tomato Bread Soup (page 154)

— Stracciatella Pizza with Spicy Roasted Tomato Sauce and Scallion (page 111)

— Escarole Salad with Lemon, Anchovy, Parmigiano-Reggiano, and Breadcrumbs (page 167)

— Buttermilk Panna Cotta with Orange Anise Compote (page 202)

ERIC LARKEE
Former Beverage Director

— Watermelon Spritz (page 220)

— Meatballs (page 138)

— Oven-Roasted Chicken Wings with Agrodolce Glaze and Rosemary Crema (page 141)

— Warm Brussels Sprouts with Burrata, Pears, Pistachios, and Creamy Parmesan Dressing (page 165)

— Margherita Pizza (page 72)

— Mushroom Pizza (page 80)

— Chocolate Chunk Cookies (page 213)

Flagship restaurant Michael's Genuine Food and Drink in the Miami Design District celebrates fresh, simple, and pure food and drink, setting the bar for ultimate neighborhood dining in Miami since 2007 with its laid-back bistro atmosphere, emphasis on sourcing seasonal ingredients, and lively bar scene and courtyard. Michael Schwartz has since developed complementary fine-dining concepts, including honest Italian at Fi'lia by Michael Schwartz at SLS Brickell in Downtown Miami (October 2016) and Baha Mar, Nassau, in the Bahamas (December 2017); the quintessential Miami waterfront restaurant with a fresh take on bold Latin American flavors at Amara at Paraiso, in the Paraiso District, East Edgewater, Miami (January 2018); and an oasis within the oasis of Miami's bohemian village, Coconut Grove, in Tigertail + Mary at Park Grove (2019).

Genuine Pizza is a casual pizza restaurant built on passion for our favorite food. Genuine Pizza is a place to enjoy a great meal with great people and without pretense, with consideration of every detail of the dining experience, from the careful selection of ingredients to the choices made in crafting dishes and the space in which you enjoy them. The seed of Genuine Pizza is Harry's Pizzeria, first opened in 2011. With inspiration from Michael Schwartz's flagship, Michael's Genuine Food & Drink, Harry's became a fixture of the Miami dining scene and a nationally recognized pizza hot spot, named one of *Food & Wine* magazine's 25 Best Pizzerias in the U.S. An evolution of the best of the original, Genuine Pizza celebrates its beloved flagship menu anchored by hand-formed pizzas featuring a tender, quick-fired crust with integrity. At the table, the experience is complete with warm service and wholesome dishes to make a meal, including snacks, colorful salads, daily specials, and dessert. From the sidewalk to the dining room, the restaurant buzzes with friends and family hanging out over craft beer, a creative wine list, and great music.

Ella Pop is a café that opened in 2015, light and airy in the Miami Design District's Palm Court, serving breakfast, lunch, small bites, freshly made pastries, and a convenient grab-and-go station. Michael Schwartz Events offers catering and private parties, with delicious food and hospitality for memorable occasions. TGHG has been recognized by leading trade magazine *Restaurant Hospitality* as one of its RH 25: Coolest Multi-Concept Companies.

233

If you are reading these acknowledgments, chances are you've read, or will read, this book. Which means we have at least one thing in common: a passion for good food. Food rules my life. It has introduced me to so many amazing people, taken me on great journeys, and provided unbelievable opportunities for my family and me.

Food brings people together; it creates, and is driven by, a desire to congregate. Cooking a meal at home and sharing it around a table with loved ones is one of the simplest and satisfying pleasures, and forms my most vivid memories. The mere whiff of a favorite dish can instantly connect us to a time, place, and feeling. For a few of us, lucky to have found a passion cooking professionally, food provides an opportunity to create and enjoy a whole new family—a restaurant family, who goes to battle with you and who you rely on, and learn from, daily; a brigade like no other, who will do anything for one another.

And for a rare few crazy enough to want to create a cookbook, there is a whole other family of inspiring, brilliant people that you may otherwise never know, but who instantly become as close a family as you could think possible.

And so, I am blessed with many families, and it is my pleasure to thank them here.

My wife, Tamara, who—in addition to being supportive and thoughtful along the journey—has taught me more about everything and anything than anyone else. Thanks, babe!

Our children: Ella, Lua, and Harry. The toughest critics and the best kids anyone could ask for!

My mother, Judy, for teaching me how to cut the bread for Thanksgiving stuffing. And being amazing. And her husband Eddie Caruso (who has such an awesome name) for taking such good care of her!

My father, Marvelous Marv, for always ordering his pizza with "lite" cheese and hammered to death. Miss you, Dad!

Sunil Bhatt, my best friend and business partner, whose passion for pizza is contagious.

Victoria Pesce Elliott for opening her beautiful home (the Schwartz family's home away from home where we spent so many days all cooking together) to us.

Restaurant Family:

The amazing, creative, connected, talented workhorse/ energizer bunny, Jackie Sayet, who does NOT stop!

The analytical and thoughtful Joel White, aka Columbo.

The better version of me (better, faster, stronger): Bradley Herron.

Dillion Wolff: the shinier, newer, younger Brad!

Brandon Green, the rookie.

Eric Larkee, the rain man and wine and beverage wiz.

Charles Bell, the big toe.

To the restaurant teams at Genuine Pizza, Harry's Pizzeria, Michael's Genuine Food and Drink, Ella Pop, and Amara at Paraiso, who all work tirelessly day-in and day-out, and not only enhance the culinary fabric of Miami—and beyond—but also make me look good each and every day!

Book Family:

Brandi Bowles, my agent, who put it all together and, most importantly, introduced us to the amazing Olga Massov.

Olga Massov, who knows more about everything than anyone I know, and how to put it into the best words!

Sidney Bensimon who, with her lens and talent, brought the book to life along with Martha Bernabe (whose Instagram stories are masterpieces) and her treasure trove of props (and her handler Mic)!

And last, but most certainly not least, über-editor Laura Dozier, art director Deb Wood, and all the talented folks at Abrams Books for preserving our voice, keeping us focused, steering the ship, and making all of this happen!

Wolfgang Puck, for sharing with me his love of unconventional pizza—and for teaching me that it's OK to get wildly imaginative with your toppings.

And, of course, to all our guests who have supported my team and me over the years so we can do what we do. It's why we do what we do.

I am not one for being overly prescriptive. Cooking should be enjoyable and you should cook with ingredients easily available, and affordable, to you. That said, some ingredients and tools are so wonderful, I feel I need to stand behind them 100 percent. Others might be tricky to locate, and so I'm listing them here, as well. Particularly with tools, the ones I list below are, in my opinion, superior to the competition, and in some cases are even more affordable than competing products.

INGREDIENTS

ANCHOVIES
Agostino Recca
Amazon.com
Whole Foods Market

CAPERS
La Nicchia
Amazon.com

CHEESES
Belgioioso
Belgioioso.com

CRUSHED CALABRIAN CHILES IN OIL
Amazon.com
Whole Foods Market

FLAKY SEA SALT
Maldon
specialty stores,
Amazon.com

FLOUR
King Arthur Flour
available in grocery stores nationwide

KOSHER SALT
Diamond Crystal
available in grocery stores nationwide

MEAT, CHICKEN, AND SALUMI
Niman Ranch
Nimanranch.com

OLIVE OIL
California Olive Ranch
available nationwide as well as online at californiaranch.com

STRACCIATELLA
specialty Italian food shops

TOOLS

IMMERSION BLENDER
Breville
Sur La Table,
Amazon.com

MANDOLINE
Benriner
Amazon.com

PEPPERMILL
Unicorn
Amazon.com

VEGETABLE Y-PEELER
Kuhn Ricon
Amazon.com (pack of three)

ZESTER
Microplane
Sur La Table,
Amazon.com

Editor: Laura Dozier
Designer: Deb Wood
Production Manager:
  Michael Kaserkie

Library of Congress Control Number:
  2018936276

ISBN: 978-1-4197-3439-7
eISBN: 978-1-68335-504-5

Printed and bound in China
10 9 8 7 6 5 4 3 2 1

Abrams books are available at special
discounts when purchased in quantity
for premiums and promotions as well
as fundraising or educational use.
Special editions can also be created
to specification. For details, contact
specialsales@abramsbooks.com or
the address below.

Abrams® is a registered trademark of
Harry N. Abrams, Inc.

ABRAMS The Art of Books
195 Broadway, New York, NY 10007
abramsbooks.com